best practice
benchmarking

Gulf Publishing Company
Houston, Texas

best practice
benchmarking
an international perspective

sylvia codling

Best Practice Benchmarking

Published in 1996 by Gulf Publishing Company under arrangement with Gower Publishing Ltd, Old Post Road, Brookfield, Vermont 05036.

Gulf Publishing Company
Book Division
P.O. Box 2608 ☐ Houston, Texas 77252-2608

10 9 8 7 6 5 4 3 2 1

Library of Congress Cataloging-in-Publication Data

Codling, Sylvia.
    Best practice benchmarking / Sylvia Codling.
      p. cm.
    Includes bibliographical references and index.
    ISBN 0-88415-134-4
    1. Benchmarking (Management)—Europe—Case studies.   2. Total quality management—Europe—Case studies.   I. Title.
    HD62.15.C565   1996
    658.5′62—dc20   96-2804
                                                       CIP

CONTENTS

ACKNOWLEDGMENT

The author and publisher wish to thank Vicki J. Powers and *Continuous Journey,* the magazine of the American Productivity and Quality Center, for several case studies included in this edition.

FOREWORD

Sylvia Codling has created a unique reference with a truly international perspective. In fact, the many international examples set this book apart from any others. It is a much-needed addition to the existing literature on benchmarking, which up until now has been almost exclusively US-oriented.

Emphasis is also given to different perspectives with the liberal use of charts and diagrams. Previous thinking on the subject is extended, particularly through inclusion of the softer, behavioral aspects of benchmarking and change management, together with the introduction of the supply chain considerations.

Best Practice Benchmarking also shows the combination of benchmarking and Total Quality Management (TQM), which is a point that needs to be stressed since benchmarking is a quality tool: the one that sources "best practices" to feed the continuous improvement efforts of TQM. The case studies will also be of interest to the reader.

There is more than adequate new material to make this a much-needed addition to the art and science of benchmarking. I always welcome new perspectives on this subject, and I warmly commend this book to the reader.

Since 1992 when I wrote the above (foreword to the first edition), *Best Practice Benchmarking* has become a benchmarking classic, serving individuals and organizations in the United Kingdom and Europe as their basic text for benchmarking. Its success has led to this edition, updated with new case material, for the North American market. Its simple, easy-to-read style should ensure an equally wide audience on this side of the "pond" where, despite arguably greater awareness of benchmarking, there is always a need to have the basics described in a straightforward manner for all newcomers to the art of this powerful technique.

Robert C. Camp Ph.D., P.E.
Manager, Benchmarking Competency
The Quality Network
Rochester, NY 14625

PREFACE

In times of rapid economic and technical change, profitability and growth come from a clear understanding of how a business is performing, not just against its own results last year but against the best it can measure.

In 1960, the *Harvard Business Review* published Theodore Levitt's landmark paper "Marketing Myopia." In this article, Levitt delivered his research findings showing that major innovations in any sector come from outside the industry. Yet many firms have continued to look internally or within their industry for clues to achieve or maintain competitive edge. In evermore sophisticated and demanding markets, the need to develop an external perspective has never been more crucial. In today's dynamic environment, benchmarking is potentially the most powerful weapon in the strategic armoury.

In North America, benchmarking first captured the imagination of corporate managers following Xerox Corporation's pioneering use of the technique in the late 1970s and early 1980s. It subsequently became a requirement of assessment for the Malcolm Baldridge Quality Award, followed in 1992 by its inclusion in the criteria for the equally prestigious European Quality Award and, in 1994, the UK Quality Award. Practical evidence that it delivers benefits is provided by the numerous organizations that have implemented benchmarking during the past two decades, a representative sample of which are included in this book.

Across industry there are examples of how benchmarking has improved performance. For example, it has helped Cummins Engine Company reduce delivery time from eight months to eight weeks; Lucas has reduced the number of shopfloor grades at one of its sites from 17 to four; British Rail has cut cleaning time for a 660-seat train to just eight minutes; and it has helped one company go from the back of the pack in its multinational group to winner of the coveted Deming Award in Japan. Elsewhere, order processing time has been reduced from weeks to just a few days, engineering drawings per man-year have doubled, and inventory has been cut by two-thirds.

In 1990, the author's organization, Oak Business Developers PLC, caried out the first national survey into benchmarking awareness and practice in the UK. At that time, the majority of managers cited lack of knowledge of the concept as the chief barrier to implementation. Since then, interest and understanding have grown and spread, and an increasing number of case studies have been published. Despite this, confusion still grows and the questions asked by those new to the technique remain the same: "What *exactly* is it?" and "How *precisely* do we do it?"

The purpose of this book is to answer these questions. It can be read quickly to provide an overview of the subject and its origins and fit within modern management. Through two chapters of snapshots and case histories, plus numerous references throughout the text, it shares the experience and knowledge gained by other benchmarking companies. Last, but by no means least, a substantial portion of the text provides a step-by-step guide to the process (with planning worksheets provided in the Appendix) for managers who want to do it for themselves.

However, a management tool should never become blunted by bureaucratic constraints and structures. Rather like the Ten Commandments, the 12-step process explained here in detail should be approached as a guiding methodology. All the steps, and their sequence, need to be fully understood to establish direction and context. Understand and learn the process, then teach, train, and develop your people so that it becomes second nature to them.

Once understood, however, benchmarking can be adapted to suit the style of both the managers and the organization. AT&T uses a 12-step process but Xerox Corporation has 10, Royal Mail has eight, Aluminum Company of America (Alcoa) has six, and TNT has five. This does not mean that these companies throw out some steps. It simply means that in practice some steps naturally combine.

Benchmarking is a flexible discipline that has become a way of life in some of the world's leading organizations. During the past decade, competitve analysis has helped companies understand and improve their relative position. Benchmarking takes over where this ends. From parity to superiority, learning from the best can help your company become the world leader in those factors imperative to its success. In so doing, you will gain an enduring and continuously improving competitive edge.

best practice
benchmarking

INTRODUCTION

Records dating back to the ancient Egyptians point to the use of benchmarks in construction work. The Egyptians cut a notch in a lump of stone at an accurately determined point, while a flat strip of iron would then be placed horizontally in the incision to act as the support (bench) for a leveling-staff. Using this as the reference (mark), further heights and distances could be measured. The tools have developed as technology has changed, but the word "benchmark" retains the same meaning in surveying and construction.

For managers and organizations, the word has long been used to denote an acceptable standard, specification, or performance. Benchmark setting then evolved as the technique whereby benchmarks (most frequently pertaining to a particular industry or sector) were identified so that companies could devise strategies to ensure they achieved that standard. Thus companies would set a "hurdle" rate of, say, the rate of inflation plus X% as the minimum acceptable return when judging capital investment proposals.

Major exponents of this technique in the UK are Profit Impact of Market Strategy (PIMS) and The Center for Interfirm Comparison (CIFC). Since the 1950s, PIMS has built up a considerable database of facts, figures, cost, and investment ratios for companies in Europe and North America. Using specialized models, PIMS can analyze a company's past and present performance. This can be compared with a spread of "look-alike" businesses in similar positions experiencing similar market growth, fluctuations, and circumstances.

Such analyses produce a picture of how a particular business compares with its peers and, more importantly, to what extent it deviates from the "benchmarks" across a number of operations and parameters, such as purchasing, marketing, research and development, administration, net income, return on investment, and so on. This comparison provides information showing how the company stands in terms of performance, and identifies areas where it is weak or strong when compared with similar businesses. This technique highlights specific areas where significant improvements would have most benefit to overall performance.

CIFC, on the other hand, adopts a similar process to determine management ratios; these show how firms compare with their competitors. The technique, however, while pin-pointing parameters, does not show *how* to improve performance.

It should be borne in mind that an analysis that looks only at the results may lead to fallible conclusions. For example, if the analysis shows the firm to be on a par with others in similar circumstances, it would lead to complacency. After all, if the target is to perform only in line with the industry standard, there is little to gain from investing to be superior.

Equally, analyses may indicate a firm's performance to be measurably below its peers in several key aspects. An investment decision to improve these areas, based only on this, may not be the wisest course of action. Take, for example, sales per employee. If this is well below the industry standard, the cause may be outdated plant equipment, overmanning, attitudes, employee morale, or many other factors. Substantial investment in a new plant will not necessarily improve the ratio. Obviously, further investigation, particularly of the intangible aspects, would be needed to uncover the real causes. Analysis of the results is not particularly helpful in such instances.

The development of the computer industry throughout the 1960s and 1970s brought a further development in the use of benchmarking.

Multiple suppliers and diverse system configurations made computer selection increasingly complex, particularly for end-users who were not always technically sophisticated. Complexities of the buying decision multiplied with the advent of an increasing supply base of personal computers, portables, laptops, and mainframes, as well as the accompanying array of software. Constantly evolving and improving, the technology facilitated ever-increasing configurations to further confuse the buyer. A number of techniques were developed to measure and compare performance. According to an article in the *MIS Quarterly* (March 1985), Byron C. Lewis (Department of Decision Sciences, Georgia State University, Atlanta) and Albert E. Crews (Data General Corporation, Alabama) stated that of the five most commonly accepted measures, only benchmarking had received consistent use as a performance evaluation tool.

Hardware and software suppliers now provide benchmark data in their systems information packages. Performance benchmarks aim to give an "appropriate idea of the kind of performance" the buyer can expect from his or her application.

In the late 1970s, benchmarking was pioneered in the realms of management practice by the Xerox Corporation in the US. At that time Xerox was losing a significant share of the lucrative photocopier market to its Japanese counterparts. Investigations showed that the Japanese could sell a unit in the US cheaper than the Americans could manufacture it. Xerox carried out exhaustive analyses of unit production costs in its manufacturing operations and compared these with Japanese counterparts. The company was fortunate in being able to enlist the assistance of Fuji Xerox, its Japanese affiliate, in this work.

Xerox discovered that production costs in the US were much higher than in Japan. The US manufacturing operatives adopted the lower Japanese costs as targets for deriving their own business plans and initiated a benchmarking process to effect the required improvements. This work resulted not only in halting the erosion of Xerox's market share but eventually helped the firm claw back the lost percentage from the Japanese.

In the world of benchmarking, Xerox's use of, and success with, the technique is now legend. It is acclaimed as one of the major factors in the company's revitalization from its declining position in the 1970s to success in the 1980s. This culminated in the company becoming a Baldrige Award winner in 1991.

Evidence such as this has led to remarkable growth in managements' use of benchmarking in the US throughout the 1980s. The technique has now been incorporated into the Application Guidelines for the Baldrige Award, with companies having to describe their approach to selection of world class benchmarks in support of strategic quality planning. Not surprisingly, companies such as AT&T, DuPont, General Electric (GE), General Motors (GM), Milliken, and Motorola all regularly apply benchmarking techniques to critical areas of their operations. Benchmarking networks have sprung up across the US specifically to share the experience and knowledge gained. AT&T undertakes regular benchmarking investigation tours across all industry sectors, willingly passing on the information and experience so achieved through reports and training courses that are also open to other companies.

The benchmarking approach to target setting is steadily gaining a toehold in Europe. Certain industry sectors, insurance for example, are familiar with benchmark setting to establish their target ratios. Companies in these sectors are moving gradually toward a continuous process of comparing themselves against their peers. Leading edge companies such as Digital Equipment Corporation, Milliken Industrials (UK), and Rank Xerox are now developing benchmarking as an integral part of corporate strategy. They are rapidly being joined by those with European parent organizations such as British Steel, British Telecom, ICL, and Shell.

In much the same way as the development of benchmarking in the US followed Total Quality Management (TQM), benchmarking is achieving a higher profile in Europe through a number of continuous improvement initiatives.

In the UK, the British Quality Foundation has a key objective to promote best practice in quality management throughout industry and commerce. It was the first organization in that country to organize a seminar, in March 1991, on the effective use of benchmarking, which included a presentation by the author on where and how benchmarking was being adopted in the UK. For the next three years, a benchmarking committee which sprang from this event worked behind the scenes to encourage and promote the technique through the Foundation's other activities. When the UK Quality Award was re-launched in 1994, benchmarking against best practice was incorporated as one of the key assessment criteria.

Through its Department of Trade and Industry (DTI), the British government has also become increasingly supportive of benchmarking as a performance measurement and improvement technique to raise the overall competitiveness of the country. In the early 1990s, this support was implicit in a program known as "Managing in the 90s." However, since 1994 it has gradually raised awareness of the concept through successive annual "Competitiveness White Papers." The 1996 edition includes information on the National Benchmarking Scheme, a framework of benchmarking services aimed at different segments of the market, but each service sharing common statistical data and providing referral between services. It is anticipated that such statistical comparison will enable calibration of services and measurement against "best in class" values.

Another new initiative launched for 1996 is the Small Firms Benchmarking Service, which will seek to raise awareness and encourage greater use of the technique to stimulate smaller companies to achieve a competitive edge. Through a national network of business advisers, it will provide a toolkit to enable assessment of business performance and suggest avenues for improvement, which may involve detailed benchmarking using a commercial service.

Benchmarking is also spreading as a direct result of its inclusion in the assessment criteria for the European Quality Award and UK Quality Award. The Business Excellence Model, around which the criteria for both awards are built, is fast becoming one of the most popular frameworks within which organizations identify performance gaps against best practice. Testimony to its effectiveness in this context is provided by the joint winners of the inaugural UK Quality Award, Rover Group Ltd, and TNT Express UK Ltd, who were two of the first companies to adopt benchmarking in that country. In fact, some of the earliest benchmarking Rover Group carried out was against TNT Express UK, which is further evidence of the mutual benefit.

A continuing request from new and practiced benchmarkers alike is for relevant case material from best practice companies of how the technique has delivered business benefit to them. Although the library of case material has grown dramatically over the past two years in response to this need in the marketplace, most organizations are still reticent to document their efforts, particularly with regard to learning points. In order to raise awareness of the need for well-documented studies as well as to reward efforts in this area, The Benchmarking Centre located in the UK launched The European Best Practice Benchmarking Award in 1995. Sponsored by leading European organizations, the award was won in its inaugural year by Hewlett Packard's Finance and Remarketing Division with IBM UK's National Call Management Centre coming a close second. Both organizations have subsequently presented their award-winning cases at numerous conferences and seminars across Europe, while The Benchmarking Centre has been inundated with requests for copies of the case study material. Over coming years, these and successive winners of The European Best Practice Benchmarking Award will continue to inspire others in their search for excellence.

In Japan, the concept of *Kaizen*, or Total Continuous Improvement, combined with *Dantotsu*—striving to be the best—has driven companies to leadership positions in many industry sectors. Firms realize that their position is vulnerable if they do not continually seek improved ways of operating, irrespective of industry or application. As many companies have learned to their cost, the threat from the East will not diminish. Some leading companies are turning to joint ventures with former arch rivals to counter the threat—and are themselves posing a threat to indigenous companies; for example, JCB's association with Sumitomo, or Rover Group's involvement with Honda and subsequently with BMW. Others are conducting international benchmarking interchanges across industry boundaries—for example, Cummins Engine Company and Komatsu Limited.

In 1989, when Robert Camp published the Xerox experience in his book *Benchmarking: The Search for Industry Best Practices that Lead to Superior Performance,* the technique was virtually unknown in Europe. Oak Business Developers' pioneering survey in the UK was closely followed by the first European text on benchmarking (the first edition of this book) in 1992. This, for the first time, provided managers with a methodology they could follow to introduce the concept of benchmarking. Since then, the library on the subject has continued to expand through the efforts of academics and practitioners alike. Consequently, with each year that passes, the technique has gained increasing recognition as one of the most powerful tools in the competitive armory. From its roots in manufacturing industry, benchmarking has spread through the service and public sectors, engaged the attention of social and welfare agencies, and tested the ingenuity of those in the health and education sectors. Also, the number of support networks continues to grow. When the UK Benchmarking Centre was launched in 1992, it was the only one in Europe. Since then it has been joined by Sweden, Italy, Germany, Finland, and France, and others are about to be launched. On a broader front, The Benchmarking Centres in Italy, Sweden, Germany, Finland, and UK are members of a 14-strong consortium, together with a number of universities and specialists in communications systems and software, sponsored by the European Commission. The main thrust of The World Class Standard Network (WCSN), as this consortium is known, is to support the transformation of European businesses through provision and promotion of technologies for dissemination of evidence of world-class practices. This will enable organizations to access a broader base of best-practice partners and information against which to benchmark.

When the first edition of this book was published in 1992 it stated that "the combination of climate, experience, and necessity now seems set to ensure the growth and development of benchmarking." The intervening years have proven the truth of that statement. Although it is still frequently referred to as a "buzzword" or "the latest fad," it shows no sign of abating. On the contrary, the author's experience is that its adoption is increasingly moving from an operational improvement tool to a major facilitator of strategic advantage and corporate change. Nor are we aware of any organization where, once benchmarking has been adopted, it has subsequently ceased to be an integral part of "the way we do things around here." It seems to have become part of the fabric of everyday life, so my guess is it's here to stay!

1

WHAT IS BENCHMARKING?

MEASURING AND IMPROVING PERFORMANCE
ESSENTIAL FOR CONTINUOUS IMPROVEMENT
AN INTEGRAL PART OF QUALITY MANAGEMENT

Benchmarking has been variously defined by dictionaries and companies. Xerox Corporation, which is the pioneer of the technique's application in management practice, defines it as: "The search for industry best practices which lead to superior performance." The key words are "best practice" and "superior performance."

Traditional competitive analyses focus on performance parameters, strategies and products within a given industry sector. Such analyses result in a picture of how a business compares with its peers and how much it deviates from the standards, or benchmarks, across any number of operations and parameters. From this, a business derives an indication of its relative standing and its comparative strengths and weaknesses. These enable it to set targets to achieve parity with the recognized industry leaders.

While such analyses have a place in corporate strategy, they have the potential to inhibit performance improvement and growth. Comparisons with look-alike businesses in similar markets and situations are unlikely to identify or lead to significant breakthroughs that could overturn the paradigms of the sector.

Instead, benchmarking is: "An *ongoing process* of measuring and improving products, services and practices against the *best* that can be identified worldwide." There are no limitations on the search; the more creative the thinking, the greater the potential reward. Unlike competitive analyses, which focus on outputs, benchmarking is applied to key operational processes within a business. It means determining the critical success factors across the organization. Processes governing those factors are analyzed. The best organizations in the world at those processes are established. These are then used to target improvements. Only a thorough understanding of in-house processes makes it possible to recognize and integrate the differences or innovations which will be found in the "best practice" companies under study.

This understanding comes from adopting a structured, rational approach provided by benchmarking. Essentially, there are four stages:

- Planning;
- Analysis;
- Action;
- Review.

While each stage is important and must be completed thoroughly, the more time spent at the planning stage, the less is likely to be wasted later on. Review is a necessary and distinct stage in its own right that also interweaves through the planning, analysis, and action phases.

There is another fundamental difference between benchmarking and traditional competitive analysis. Whereas the latter has a suggestion of "cloak-and-dagger" in its methods of data gathering, often employing industrial "spies," benchmarking depends for its success on cooperation between partners.

THREE TYPES OF BENCHMARKING

This need to look for cooperative partnerships has led to the evolution of three distinct "types" or "perspectives" on benchmarking:

- Internal;
- External;
- Best practice.

INTERNAL BENCHMARKING

This refers to partners within your company, or division, who may be based at the same, or a different location. So, for example, if you have identified processes dealing with customer complaint handling, you could compare practices across different sales departments if they exist on the same site or those at a number of geographically dispersed offices or locations.

Many companies, when they begin benchmarking, start by looking for internal comparisons. There are some good reasons for this, not the least of which is that data are collected relatively easily. Also, the culture and language are the same, surroundings are familiar, communication channels exist, management know each other, and so on.

Internal benchmarking can be seen as the "nursery" for developing the approach. Processes can be analyzed, questions asked, and mistakes made in a relatively unthreatening environment. It can provide, therefore, a sound learning base for the technique. Although internal comparison are unlikely to result in major breakthroughs, they will probably result in "adequate" returns. Moreover, the results can be effected relatively quickly. If enthusiasm and commitment to the approach are less than overwhelming in the organization, early small gains from internal benchmarking may provide a necessary injection of energy into the system. In many cases, significant savings do result from the process analysis involved.

One of the side effects of increased globalization is the move toward harmonization on best practice, methods, or systems existing across a company's world operations. This has happened, for example, at Johnson Group Cleaners (which has 25% of the British market and 2% of the massive North American market—including the biggest US chain). "The first thing we do (when acquiring a business) is standardize accounting systems immediately," the chairman said recently. "The sharing of information between our companies tends to bring out a system of best practice quite naturally."

Unilever has adopted the approach to monitor and compare costs across its subsidiaries. While highlighting areas of greater cost efficiency, it is also challenging long-established habits and practices, leading to even greater cost reductions as processes are refined. For example, fish fingers, which are available currently in seven sizes, in the future will be made in only two sizes while the number of margarine tub sizes will be reduced from 19 to nine.

Traditional monitoring systems tend not to highlight duplications and anomalies. A budget exercise that seeks a regular and constant improvement in return rarely demands that managers examine the processes involved. Quite often things "happen" simply through local custom and habit built up over a number of years. Under the old-style management, perhaps there was no reason for a manager in one country to ask how something was done at one of the locations of the business in another country. The process focus inherent in benchmarking forces managers to identify each step and, by comparison, learn precisely where savings can be made.

EXTERNAL BENCHMARKING

Many companies progress from internal to external benchmarking. External partners may be found within your group (in a multinational corporation) but in a different business division. However, they may come from completely different companies within different industries. The fact that the products differ is a benefit rather than a disadvantage because the problems that surround competitive benchmarking can be largely avoided.

The advantage of benchmarking, which looks at processes rather than outputs, is that many diverse businesses share a certain number of general major league processes (those essential to run the business) such as warehousing, distribution, manufacturing, and an even greater number of minor league processes (the myriad supports) such as telephone answering, paper handling, accident recording, customer service, and so on.

Going beyond discrete product evaluations, benchmarking does more than quantify performance gaps. Although hard processes are compared, an essential part of the approach is the necessity to analyze the management skills and attitudes that combine to make the systems operate effectively. This hidden narrative is as important during the benchmarking exercise as are the visible factors. Often it is a combination of similar processes/different attitudes that determines "best" practice and may lead to new ways of operating, better use of resources and even process innovations.

The more externally focused the benchmarking exercise, the greater the potential for removing blinkers, overturning paradigms, and overcoming the "not-invented-here" syndrome. All too often, progress is hampered by the misplaced belief that something "won't work in this industry because . . ." The "because" is frequently "we don't" or "can't do things that way because we're different." It is an unfortunate conceit of human beings that they tend to believe, for whatever reason, that "we know better." Benchmarking teaches that no single person or company has a monopoly on all the good ideas. It is always possible to learn from someone else.

Recently, much emphasis has been placed, particularly in management articles, on the competitive advantage to be gained from benchmarking. However, the disadvantages of trying to work with direct competitors by far outweigh the advantages.

The most obvious reason is that competitors are unlikely to enter a dialogue with each other, particularly concerning products or processes that are directly competitive. Other problems, such as legal constraints and ethical considerations (perceived collusion, for example) also make such dialogue difficult. Also there is the question of whether a competitor can be trusted not to feed misinformation.

Nonetheless, there may be occasions when it is necessary or desirable to consider benchmarking with a competitor. The objective still remains to build a cooperative, ongoing relationship. With this in mind, the first step, given an agreement in principle, is to set down a clear legal framework within which it is agreed to work. The information that *is* to be shared, and that which is *not* available, should be defined clearly, leaving no room for ambiguity or future misunderstanding. Once such an agreement is in place, the benchmarking exercise can begin.

There are instances when competitive benchmarking can be highly beneficial. This may apply, for example, where the process in question is one which is particularly critical to an industry. A good example is health and safety in the chemical industry. DuPont is recognized as the "best" in this area and has no problem sharing information with other companies, whether in the chemical sector or not. In reality, it is a positive benefit that can ensure the operations in their industry continue to be acceptable to an increasingly environment-conscious society.

In summary, external benchmarking is conducted between:

• Partners in different industries but the same group of companies, as in the case of large multinationals;
• Partners in different industry sectors but sharing similar processes.

Direct competitors should only benchmark with each other in very specific circumstances, where a process is unique to the industry, for example, or where very clearly defined guidelines are agreed upon from the outset.

BEST PRACTICE BENCHMARKING

Benchmarking against best practice requires seeking out the undisputed leader in the process that is critical to business success—regardless of sector or location. The problem is not just to find the "best" but to define what this means in terms of the process being examined. There are many different perceptions of "best" according to what is being considered.

Imagine, for example, you are trying to decide which is the best car to buy. You would probably consider what it was most frequently to be used for—shopping or to provide rapid transport from home to office; whether a family car with ample room for children and pets or mainly a one-person transport; how important are factors like safety and fuel consumption and so on. Having defined what influences the decision, you can then draw up a short list of models to look at closely. You are then unlikely to waste time looking at a Ferrari if what you need is a small, economical, easily parked car to do the household shopping.

The procedure is similar in business. In the case of best "telephone response to customers," it could be that the "fastest" response, or the "most polite" or "most helpful" could be defined as the best. The more complex the subject area, the greater attention that must be given to defining the terminology to ensure that Rolls-Royce cars will not be measured against Ford Escorts.

Subsequent chapters consider in more detail the importance of defining accurately each word that is used to describe the process under examination, so that each individual fully understands.

At this stage, it is sufficient to appreciate that there is no single "best" practice company. Nor may the partner for one company necessarily be the "best" for another. A single company may be the "best" practice partner for a number of others for the same or a variety of processes. The combinations are numerous.

For this reason, the "best" company to benchmark against will not be found merely by asking a person in another company that is benchmarking its processes. That company is unlikely to have precisely the same considerations. There are no easy answers. The only way to discover which company is "best" for your organization is to go through planning and data collection systematically and thoroughly.

Because the definition of which process or which company is complicated, and it may take a long time to gather the data, few companies begin their benchmarking experience at this point. Generally speaking, companies will "practice" with internal partners, progress to "external" better practice partners and only gradually build up to benchmarking against the "best."

In the early stages of best practice benchmarking, it is important to find a partner that is measurably better in the process that needs to be improved. Once the partner's performance has been matched and (since the aim is superiority, not parity) exceeded, the exercise may be repeated as the search for a still "better" partner or partners continues. Each exercise must be seen as a progression of steps leading to the ultimate "best." There is no shortcut.

To quote T. S. Eliot: "Our ends do not know our beginnings." If it is believed from the outset that the "best" partner will be the first partner, then immediately this could be the first mistake. Perserverance and practice lead to the "best." The motivator is that, of the three described approaches, best practice benchmarking provides the opportunity to make the most significant improvement and the highest increase on returns, and has the greatest potential for major breakthroughs.

2

WHY COMPANIES NEED BENCHMARKING

STRIVING FOR SUPERIORITY
IMPACT OF EXTERNAL CONDITIONS
GIVES FOCUS TO PROCESSES

If they are to be effective, business tools and techniques must be suited to the climate and culture in which companies are operating. Benchmarking provides organizations with a focus on the external environment and an emphasis on increasing process efficiency. In the present climate of dynamic change and fiercely competitive markets, both of these are essential for survival.

Change is not new; ability to handle change effectively has always been a feature of management. The difference lies in the pace (see Figure 2.1). In the field of technology, for example, where progress feeds on itself to fuel further advances, rapid movement is perhaps to be expected. However, technology has to be directed and driven to meet customer needs. For example, increasing the power of passenger cars requires improved levels of safety, including shorter stopping distances. This in turn has led to the development of anti-lock brakes.

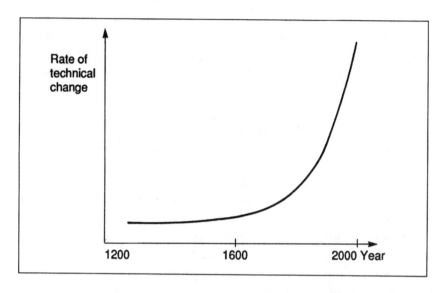

FIGURE 2.1: The evolution of technical change

There are more technologists and scientists working in the world today than during the sum total of human existence. Products are changing ever more rapidly, even if their function remains the same. Consider the development of the television since the 1950s, illustrated in Figure 2.2.

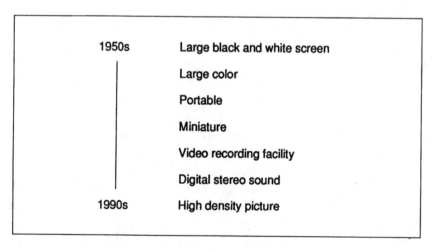

FIGURE 2.2: Changes in television technology

However, change is due not only to technological developments but also to political and demographic factors. It is imperative that business-people keep their fingers on the pulse in order to gauge the effects of change on their operations and planning. This is not unique to the present time; what provides the difference is:

- The speed at which change in one part of the world affects another part, due largely to advances in communications technology (e.g., facsimile machines).
- Information technology has made a plethora of data available to orga-nizations, pressure groups and government bodies. Factors that a few years ago were of little or no relevance, today impinge on companies and have a major impact on how they operate.

Examples of this can be found in the dramatic political shifts resulting from the breakdown of communism (in the former USSR and East Ger-many), socialism (in Sweden), and apartheid (in South Africa). Mass com-munications enable political shifts in one country to impact almost imme-diately on activities in another. The Russian revolution of 1917 may have had little impact on life in America. But a return to "democracy" in the former USSR in the 1990s has undermined the rationale for mass spend-ing on defense across the world. Two factors—the increase in America's unemployment figures and the restructuring of the British Armed Forces—are arguably attributable to this, at least in some measure.

Another example lies in the demographic and social trends that create new demands and generate significant opportunities (see Figure 2.3). A generation has grown up without the wastage of war. Women join the employment pool and stay there with only brief absences for pregnancy and childbirth. More people of employable age are chasing work, while technology is removing many of the old manual jobs and replacing them with a demand for skilled, knowledgeable workers.

In the western developed nations and Japan, there are more elderly peo-ple, thanks to the development of health services and pharmaceuticals. At the other end of the cycle, children are being born to older parents and stay in school longer. In percentage terms, fewer people in the work force will be supporting an increasing proportion of dependents. Social security and pensions provision will become increasingly difficult issues, while the cost of education and re-education has serious implications for the orga-nization of the future.

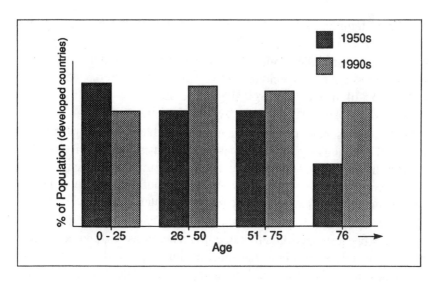

FIGURE 2.3: Demographic trends

Changes on the social front include the restyling of the traditional family; an increase in the number of one-parent households or those where the children in the same family unit have different parents; more working sin-

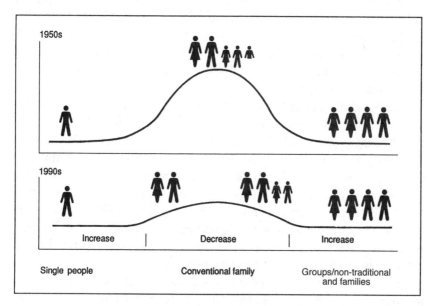

FIGURE 2.4: Societal change—distribution curve

gle parent families and an increase in the numbers of latch-key children (see Figure 2.4).

A trend that straddles political and social spheres is the increasing concern for protection of the environment. This used to be considered a preoccupation of fringe or marginal groups, but it has rapidly grown to become one of key issues in strategy and planning.

Added to this, new industries are growing up based on computers, electronics, biotechnology, and information. The business world is bombarded with novel terms—flexible manufacturing, simultaneous engineering, niche markets, just-in-time delivery and manufacturing, total process management, total cost down, electronic data interchange, etc.

These changes, shifts, and trends must be taken into consideration by managers because they directly affect the needs, desires, and perceptions of the consumers on whom the organization depends for its existence. Strategies must, therefore, be formulated in the context of the interrelationship between the organization, the consumer, and the environment.

FOCUS ON THE EXTERNAL ENVIRONMENT

This interdependence is a relatively new phenomenon but is increasing in importance. For much of the twentieth century, businesses grew without having to concern themselves too much with the outside world. Obviously, they had to take government policies and the economy into consideration when formulating plans, but other than that, strategy was based mainly on internal, production-led factors.

A major shift in attitude came about during the 1960s. A generation of young people grew up with buying decisions based not solely on the fact that something was available. They wanted choice, variety, novelty, color and innovation. As marketing developed into an essential business function, the department took on the role of the chief link between the company and the outside world. Through activities such as market research, public relations, and advertising, it was responsible for dialogue with consumers, as well as the image the company wanted to project. Business plans, however, were still production led. The organization's activities continued to be governed by internal issues, concerns, and objectives.

The traditional budgetary process is a clear example of the emphasis on looking inward rather than outward. Targets for the coming year based on past performance plus, say 5%, or on some industry average, are still common even today. Such arbitrary figures bear little relation to external factors and, in a period of rapid change, are meaningless.

Why should "We've always done it this way" be a reason for doing something? In a rapidly changing world, this can lead to extinction.

The number and extent of changes today mean that no person or business can afford to be complacent. The blinders have to be removed and thrown away. The paradigms, or frames of reference, of the past are little guide to behavior in the future. When a paradigm shift occurs, whole markets are affected. Consider the effect on candle makers of the development of gas lighting. Even this was quickly subsumed by electric lighting. Another frequently cited example is the development of quartz watches, which reduced Swiss dominance of the market for watches overnight and for many years thereafter.

A wide perspective is necessary to take into account developments and opportunities elsewhere that could fundamentally alter the shape and direction of the market. External focus, which is a prerequisite for benchmarking, coupled with ongoing and structured data gathering, is one way to keep up with the pace of change. Focusing on processes is another.

GIVING FOCUS TO PROCESS

Many companies devote considerable time and resources to purchasing and stripping other companies' products down to the minutest detail. Then they rebuild them. This is known as reverse engineering. No matter how sophisticated in application, it can show only the components of a product. It provides little information on how parts were put together and scant insight into the equipment used, or order of assembly. It is a useful, but limited, tool.

Studying the process whereby products or materials are produced is more informative. For example, two pianists in the Tchaikovsky Competition, given the same piano, music, surroundings, stool and audience, will produce two quite different performances. Only one will win. It is not the piece being played but the way (technique and style) it is played that makes the difference. Only another pianist will be able to understand precisely what distinguishes the two.

In benchmarking it is not sufficient to look only at the product. It is necessary to explore the tangible and intangible factors that combine to produce a superior performance and to involve those people most directly concerned in the activity being examined. Japanese managers, who understand this, spend some 40% of their time studying and refining processes.

Elsewhere, those who have been benchmarking for any length of time confirm that significant and early gains result from this analysis. Finding a better way to conduct a process can provide the psychological motivation for change. It leads to the acceptance that a different paradigm is possible and, indeed, desirable.

In a complex, dynamic, fast-changing environment, companies must strive for superiority in their core activities in order to survive. Competitive edge cannot be achieved or maintained by setting goals based on past or even present performance. Benchmarking itself is a process that helps identify, compare, and emulate best practice wherever it occurs. Benchmarking is essential to every company as part of the process of continuous improvement. And it has the merit that all aspects of business performance can be raised from the first point of contact (the switchboard, perhaps) to final delivery of the product.

BENCHMARKING AND CHANGE

Benchmarking promotes the climate for change:
- The gap between present and best practice promotes dissatisfaction and desire for change.
- Seeing, understanding, and learning from best practice helps to identify what and how to change.
- Witnessing best practice provides a realistic, achievable picture of the desired future.

3

WHEN AND WHERE BENCHMARKING 'FITS'

TOTAL QUALITY MANAGEMENT IS THE GOAL
QUALITY IMPROVEMENTS IDENTIFIED
PROBLEM SOLVING UNDERSTOOD

During the first half of the twentieth century, spurred by shortages resulting from wars, the need to manufacture mass quantities of staple goods spawned large industrial units. These required considerable up-front capital investment. Economies of scale and the need to minimize unit costs were governing factors in the way the organization was designed and operated.

Production was king and the customer, if considered at all, was an ignorant nuisance who could be easily manipulated: "The customer is an object to be manipulated, not a concrete person whose aims the businessman is interested to satisfy" (Erich Fromm, *Escape from Freedom,* 1941). The system encouraged hierarchical management and bureaucratic structures, a trend reinforced by growing numbers of holding companies and diversified conglomerates.

The birth of marketing in the 1960s heralded a major change in organizational structure and shape. Over the following 20 years, recognition of market needs compelled attention to switch from production-led units to customer-driven operations. Consideration turned to manufacturing flexibility, changing fashions, and awareness of concepts such as "small is beautiful" and "niche markets." To maintain and grow market share, companies had to deliver what the consumer would buy rather than what factories wanted to produce. Vertical and horizontal integration faded as the need for market responsiveness grew.

TAXING MATTERS

Vic Tishers was a self-employed management training coordinator. His tax returns were lodged with the local office by his accountant, and every year he looked with despair toward the interminable wait and frustration that ensued as his affairs were queried, checked, and double checked. It puzzled him that the Tax Office was pretty quick to make demands yet took ages to return repayments.

On such occasions, telephone conversations with the officer dealing with his file always led him to believe that matters were being resolved "as quickly as possible." His perception of "quickly" was apparently at variance with the officer's.

Finally, when patience was wearing thin, a "Tax Payers' Charter" dropped through his mailbox. It prompted him to ask his local tax inspector if he might conduct a small experiment. After discussions it was agreed that one of the clerks would monitor the progress of 10 repayment requests through the normal channels. Two factors were to be measured: time taken for the paperwork to pass through the system from receipt to signing off, and time, in minutes, that each repayment request was actually being dealt with by clerks or officers.

At the end of the experiment, the times were averaged out. Paperwork took 28 days to pass through the system; actual time spent on dealing with the forms was 30 minutes. The root causes were identified as delays occasioned through part-time working and the necessity for countersigning assessments, authorizations, and checks. Consequently, paperwork spent most of its life sitting in "in-trays" waiting to be dealt with.

Armed with this information the Tax Office was able to implement remedies which significantly reduced delays.*

---

* This fictitious parable is an amalgamation of aprocryphal comments and should not be construed as referring to any single person or place.

During the 1980s, another change was taking place. Global markets and increasing customer sophistication switched attention in the organization from "markets" to the unique nature of individuals who comprised them. The concept of quality underwent several changes as it became less something to be controlled than an intrinsic personal element in goods and services. This became a deciding factor in maintaining and growing market share.

Appreciation of the perceptual nature of quality underlined the importance of moving as close as possible to the customer. This was accompanied by stripping out unnecessary activities and concentrating on key strengths.

Organizations adopted a flatter structure to quicken responsiveness to customer needs: "Only those who become attached to their customers, figuratively and literally, and who move most aggressively to create new markets . . . will survive" (Tom Peters, *Thriving on Chaos,* 1987).

By the end of the 1980s, a combination of increasingly sophisticated customers and economic recession in many countries made markets extremely fierce, and gaining significant competitive edge became a constant battle.

Any customer of a bureaucratic organization knows that frustrations are frequently caused by lack of authority or responsibility at the point of contact. Problems or queries have to be passed across a number of desks or departments and are subjected to delays and varying priorities at each stage. Customers wait days or weeks for a piece of paper or a response that actually takes only a matter of minutes to process.

In many cases, moving closer to the customer and understanding customer needs involves empowering employees to ask questions, deal with queries, and solve problems. The need for speedier response at every stage increases the need for education in problem analysis and solving techniques.

In recent years, the concept of quality has broadened to incorporate every aspect of business operations. In other words, TQM is now the goal. The emphasis is on customer delight and speedier response at every stage of the company-customer relationship.

TQM devolves to individuals the responsibility for improving the service they give their customers, whether these are internal (i.e. within the same department or company) or external. In broad terms, improvements come from asking what is required by those being served, then analyzing how far activities or products meet these requirements. The check question is: "Are they fit for purpose?" If there is a discrepancy, appropriate corrections and improvements are sought and implemented.

Simple problems can be solved relatively quickly. Obscure problems, however, often require detailed analysis by cross-functional teams to unravel the intricate web of interconnecting factors before symptoms can be cleared away and firm foundations for action detected.

Problem-solving processes provide a structured, systematic team approach to identify and analyze root causes, breaking each down to small parts to make it more manageable. The process involves identifying, evaluating, and implementing solutions. Review is built in to ensure that the actions implemented have solved the problem successfully (see Figure 3.1). Often referred to as "plan-do-check," this discipline and the team approach required in analysis and evaluation are similar to that applied in the benchmarking process.

There comes a point, however, when further improvement becomes difficult without reference to the extrinsic environment. TQM ensures that everything is "fit for purpose" but, other than through customer surveys, provides little feedback from the outside world. An external view of who is doing what, and how, can provide renewed energy, impetus, and direction for improvement.

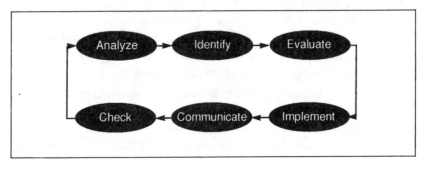

FIGURE 3.1: The basic problem solving model

This example shows where benchmarking dovetails in to the organization's quality and problem solving activities. Although in theory any company can implement it, whether going down the TQM route or not, in practice the more that quality is ingrained, the easier it is for people to relate to benchmarking. Certainly, it helps if some of the basics are in place. Aspects of Statistical Process Control or BS5750/ISO9000 systems criteria, for example, indicate a readiness to tackle the issues.

Total Quality Management is a long-term commitment. It is a powerful force for change and begins to open the windows to the world. However,

GROUNDS FOR IMPROVEMENT . . .

A company manufactures boiler tubes at two plants—one in Scotland and another in the US. The person responsible for the cylindrical grinding operation in Scotland heard that his North American counterpart performed the same operation twice as fast. Spurred by this, the Scottish operative used all the quality improvement processes he knew to improve to a speed which was one-and-a-half times that of his American counterpart.

Unable to cut the time further, he arranged to visit the US plant. As soon as he walked into the workshop he spotted the reason for the performance difference. In Scotland only one grinding head was used to run the full length of the tube. In the US two grinding heads were used to run from either end and meet in the middle. The Scotsman returned home, added another head to his machine, and managed to produce the parts in less than 75% of the time taken by his American counterpart.

it has limited ability to monitor developments outside a specific industry sector. Taking some of the tools of quality improvement and problem solving and developing them into the rigorous benchmarking process adds the external dimension that, over time, provides a cutting edge to achieve competitive superiority (see Figure 3.2).

The TQM culture influences the way in which benchmarking develops in the organization. AT&T, for example, which implemented a successful benchmarking program, found that teams with a clear view of the organization's mission and the customer's needs that must be served are more centered and confident in their activities. With this basic understanding, they encounter less of a struggle in focusing their efforts to produce usable results or actionable recommendations. Emphasis on these factors grows as organizations progress along the benchmarking learning curve. In the early states, it is better to seed confidence in the technique rather than over-control initiatives. Numerous small improvements result from internal benchmarking exercises; the greater their number, the more readily confidence in applying the technique will develop.

However, as progress is made and people become more familiar with the application, there are greater benefits to be gained from directing ener-

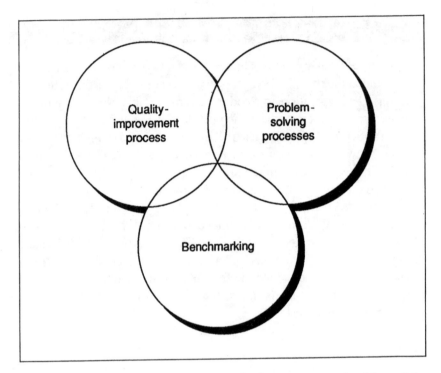

FIGURE 3.2: The benchmarking fit with quality improvement and problem solving

gies to the few factors that have greatest significance to the overall performance of the business. This is important before external benchmarking activity begins.

Top-level commitment is influential in ensuring that efforts are directed at areas of strategic importance to the business rather than those that are "nice" or "easy" to deal with. A corporate perspective provides alignment of activities with core values and keeps the ultimate goal in sight. One positive aspect of recession is the focus it gives to critical success factors that organizations have adopted to survive or remain competitive. This is central to best practice benchmarking.

Benchmarking's process focus opens the door into sectors a business would not normally consider accessible or relevant for comparison. Suddenly it becomes possible to adopt a much broader perspective. Think how different the road network looks to a pilot from 35,000 feet up in an airplane compared with when he or she is traveling by car. In much the same way, a similar focus in business can identify connections and potential diversions or blocks that could significantly affect a market or industry sector.

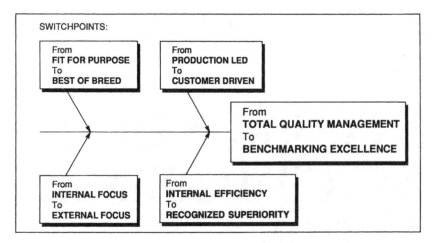

FIGURE 3.3: Impact of benchmarking on TQM

After all, even a company that is number one in its industry could see the whole business wiped out by the advent of a technology that makes the sector irrelevant. The conclusion to the boiler tube manufacturer's story makes this point clear.

Benchmarking first forces analysis of the process to hone it as far as possible, stripping out unnecessary layers, duplications and re-works. Speedier delivery at the requisite quality for the customer is the target. Then it provides the perspective whereby comparison can be made with other companies, industry sectors, and geographic locations to identify the significant improvements that can lead to optimum effectiveness. The result? Delighted customers and superior profit performance in the business's core activities and processes (see Figure 3.3).

. . . GROUNDED

The Scottish and American plant operatives mentioned earlier in this chapter continued to vie with and challenge each other to further process improvements. Some time later, despite this, both plants started to lose significant market share. While they had been busy improving against each other, a Japanese competitor developed and transformed the original process to eliminate the need to grind altogether.

4

SNAPSHOTS OF BENCHMARKING IN ACTION

WELL ESTABLISHED IN US

THE 'BROKEN ARM' SYNDROME

THE NEED FOR NETWORKS

Most companies that have had benchmarking programs in place for any length of time are either based in the US or of North American origin, and now the practice is spreading throughout Europe. They have considerable experience in the technique and provide valuable lessons.

With implementing any new technique or approach, it is difficult at first to gather enough comparable information to begin work. As the number of companies progressing along the learning curve increases, however, this problem is reduced. The "broken arm" syndrome also applies: if your arm is in plaster it is amazing how many other people you notice also wearing plaster casts. Equally, once a manager broaches the subject of benchmarking, it is surprising how many others around the table have something to contribute to the debate.

One of the most effective ways of stimulating the debate is through the development of networks. In the US, where people tend to be more free with sharing information, these have proved an effective way of spreading benchmarking philosophy and experience. Some embryonic groups are being formed in Europe, and it is only a matter of time before they, too, become effective networks.

Those that have started and are growing have provided some valuable lessons in network building. Remembering that the purpose is not to create more work but to work more effectively:

- Fix a clear purpose for each meeting and elect a chairman in advance;
- Share the workload by rotating venues between the participating companies' locations;
- Circulate relevant notes and fix the next date and agenda before everyone leaves the present meeting;
- Be prepared to give and take in equal measure.

In benchmarking, a piece of information is like an idea; the more it is shared the more it grows.

A number of companies have reported significant benefits from the use of benchmarking. These suggest that positive gains have been made, although the results can take some time to come through. The examples given here have been accumulated over a period of years from a mix of "documents in the public domain" and discussions with organizations that have faced these issues. These experiences should inspire many of those standing on the threshold of benchmarking to take the first positive step along this particular path to continuous improvement and ultimate "best" performance.

BENCHMARKING CASE STUDIES

SIEMENS PLESSEY DEFENCE SYSTEMS

In its early stages, benchmarking is often internal and informal. This may be because the company has not moved far enough down the TQM path to be "ready" for a formal program. Often called "harmonization" of best methods or practice within a company, this can make a worthwhile difference in the way a company operates. The following is one such case.

Siemens Plessey Defence Systems, based in Christchurch, is familiar with the reasoning behind benchmarking. However, it considers that a formal process is not possible until the concepts of TQM are firmly understood and implemented. Nonetheless, since being taken over by Siemens of Germany, it has initiated inter-site harmonization. The purpose of this is to ensure that processes used across the restructured company will emulate the best practice existing at any location within the new group.

LUCAS INDUSTRIES

Sometimes the seeds of benchmarking can be seen in other TQM initiatives. Consider the case of Lucas Industries.

In 1984, the management at Lucas decided that dramatic action was needed if the company was not to go the way of its Birmingham neighbor, Dunlop. The chairman and his team developed a system called "Competitiveness Achievement Plans," in which each business manager had to identify the best internal "rival" anywhere in the world and draw up a plan to close the gap between the Lucas factory and the rival.

In one instance, comparisons were made between the Lucas Heavy Duty Braking Systems plant at Cwmbran and the Lucas Car Braking Systems plant in Koblenz in Germany. Comparing the reward and remuneration systems, for example, led to the number of shopfloor grades at Cwmbran being reduced from 17 to four. In a related exercise, the number of annual pay negotiations has been reduced from five to two.

VOLKSWAGEN

Many activities become the subject of benchmarking as a result of an inadvertent comment or casual observation. In such instances, the exercise proceeds without any formal partnership or working arrangement. This was the case some years ago at Volkswagen in Germany, which now has a product agreement with Toyota in Japan.

The managing director of a Japanese car company was on a visit to Volkswagen in Germany. While there, he discovered that set-up times on their Schuller 1,000-ton press took two hours. Knowing that the same process, using the same machines, occupied four hours in his own factory, he was considerably impressed.

On his return to Japan he challenged his managers to reduce the time to a figure below that of the Volkswagen factory. To help them with this, they enlisted the help of a former chief industrial engineer with Toyota. Six months of hard work followed, but by the end of this period the team had managed to reduce the changeover time to 90 minutes.

For awhile everyone was happy. Three months later, however, the managing director issued a further challenge: The changeover time should be brought down to just three minutes!

Such a bold goal seemed impossible. The team had achieved what they considered the best possible time already using traditional methods. To meet the new target, they were forced to re-analyze and to rethink the entire changeover process and devise a significantly different approach.

Challenging the prevailing paradigms introduced them to a new concept—to externalize much of the changeover work. This meant that the work left to do during machine stoppage time was cut to a minimum. Dies, for example, could be prepared in advance, and bolt-clamping mechanisms could be simplified; meanwhile tools could be kept close at hand.

Within three months, the three-minute changeover was achieved. Now known as the SMED (Single Minute Exchange of Die) concept, it is an approach that is widely used around the world.

This is a good example of how one senior manager can personally drive the organization toward superior performance. Recognizing that another group is better at a critical process is the first step; challenging their performance is the second; and achieving a better result provides the energy and confidence to drive toward a really bold goal.

Had the managing director simply told his managers, when he returned from Germany, that he expected them to cut changeover time from four hours to three minutes they would probably have been thoroughly demoralized. As it was, he let them prove to themselves that they could achieve a better performance than had been possible elsewhere. They then felt inspired to accept the renewed challenge when it came.

BRITISH RAIL

The first steps into external benchmarking can be as informal as early internal exercises. "Keep it simple" is a good way to dip toes into the water and gather experience in the technique.

British Rail's Network South East division conducted a customer survey that showed that cleanliness is second only to punctuality in its customers' priorities. Aware that its record in this area had been unsatisfactory, it sought out the best practice.

Eventually, this was located at British Airways where it took 11 people just nine minutes to clean through a 250-seat jumbo jet. With this target in mind, British Rail developed ways to improve the efficiency of its own cleaning process. The result: It now takes British Rail cleaners eight minutes to clean up a 12-coach, 660-seat train.

CUMMINS ENGINE COMPANY

It is more useful that external benchmarking proceeds as a formal partnership where both sides are agreed on the purpose and schematic. An instance at Cummins Engine Company is a good example.

Cummins Engine Company makes marine diesel engines. It used to quote eight months from date of order to delivery. When the recession began to close in, Cummins found it was losing business to competitors. It decided to start benchmarking its processes.

One of the most critical areas, in terms of order response times, was found to be assembly on its production lines. Its information-gathering processes led it to Komatsu, which produces heavy earth moving equipment. From what it learned, prior to contacting Komatsu, the Cummins team was satisfied that the assembly processes were sufficiently similar to make benchmarking a viable possibility. The team also had evidence that Komatsu's record was significantly better than that of Cummins.

Following the initial contact, when Komatsu agreed in principle to cooperate as a partner, discussion groups were set up and within a relatively short space of time, the benchmarking plan was in place.

A major part of the cooperation involved a five-man team traveling from the UK to Japan. There the team spent several months mapping Komatsu's processes and comparing them with the processes at Cummins. Following its return to England, the team began to initiate some of the modifications it had discovered while at Komatsu. Over the next 12 months, delivery time was cut from the original eight months to eight weeks. During this time, several other improvements were "discovered," and these were fed back to the Japanese partner.

Over the next 12-month period, as a result of further modifications to interrelated processes, delivery time was reduced further to eight days. In addition, working capital was reduced to 25% of that in place before benchmarking, and the company's market share had been doubled. Furthermore, premium prices could be demanded in some market sectors because of the rapid delivery time compared with the competition.

General Electric

In most cases, benchmarking is introduced to improve the performance of factors that directly affect the bottom line—more efficient warehousing or distribution, for example. However, there are instances where the hidden benefits are at least as keen a motivator. Take, for example, the situation at General Electric (GE).

To counter the tendency toward insularity and parochialism that can be fostered easily in a large organization, the chief executive officer at General Electric introduced a global best practices program during the latter half of the 1980s.

This required that managers identified companies across the world that are better at specific aspects of business. They then sought permission to pick the brains of these practitioners. In return, GE promised to share with the better practice companies the knowledge it gained. This effectively amounted to providing free management consultancy services. Direct competitors were deliberately excluded from this program. When approached by GE to take part, few companies refused and most were flattered to be asked.

In this way, the company approached Ford for ideas on new product development and employee involvement; visited Hewlett Packard for supplier partnership and quality improvement ideas; looked to Digital Equipment for asset management ideas; studied American Express for new ideas on customer satisfaction; and investigated Honda for product development initiatives.

An integral part of GE's program is the site visits made to chosen partner companies. Teams for these generally involve no more than 10 people. Case studies built up through the visits are widely disseminated through the company as well as being included in the curriculum at GE's management development school.

Many advances have been made under this program, but GE adds a cautionary note: The "best practices" approach cannot address weaknesses until the company is ready to acknowledge that they exist.

Choosing suitable subjects

Commitment and ability to act on findings are prerequisites before any subject is placed under the microscope, otherwise the approach backfires and people become demotivated. The lesson is to not benchmark controversial or political subjects. These could include, for example, the number of female graduates retained after a given period, or the number of foreign representatives on the boards of global companies. There is little point gathering information about issues the company is unable or unwilling to resolve.

The focus should first and foremost be on critical areas of the business' operations. This is not to say that the technique cannot be used to address difficult issues, only that commitment and willingness to change must be present. The more difficult the issue the greater the commitment that is required.

The previous examples show how companies can benefit significantly from cooperating with non-competitive partners. A senior manager at Johnson & Johnson has estimated that this is where 90% of the opportunities for improvement lie, yet 90% of benchmarking companies look only at direct competitors.

There are instances where competitive benchmarking may be beneficial, but these tend not to be in areas that lead to significant edge over the competition. Suitable areas include health and safety, for example, where improving against best practice will be to the advantage of the industry as a whole. DuPont, for example, is a recognized leader in health and safety practice and has become the role model for direct competitors as well as for companies outside its sector. Other subject areas for useful competitive benchmarking are environmental protection, pollution control, community support; in other words, factors that concern industry as a whole.

As a general rule, however, it is advisable to avoid benchmarking against direct competitors. Many companies are imbued with a culture that believes in mistrusting and misleading the competition. How can the team be sure the information it is given is correct?

There is also the disadvantage that comparing practices with another company with closely resembled products may provide a blind to potential trouble spots or new rivals. The biggest and most sudden threats often come from entrants that are not constrained by the paradigms of the industry. While being intent on trying to improve a process against a competitor, others may well come along with a system that does away with the need for it altogether.

Nonetheless, competitive benchmarking is still pursued by some, as the following short examples show.

COMPETITIVE BENCHMARKING

In the late 1980s a large North American manufacturer of vehicle engines began to lose market share. It received poor engineering ratings from customers and could not understand why.

It took the decision to benchmark its competitors' engineering departments, asking customers specifically what they liked about the competitors' engineering and what they did not like about the company's approach. They also employed a specialist firm to find out, by directly asking the question: "How do competitors allocate their engineers?" This firm knew that the solution lay in casting the net wide: Half the sample contacted usually can be relied on to give information. The larger the sample, the more information is gathered. Through this form of benchmarking, the engine manufacturer found that the most successful companies assigned up to 200 of their engineers to work full time at their customers' car factories. By contrast, it allocated only 10 engineers to work directly with customers.

Although the engine manufacturer had been aware that the competition adopted this approach, they were not aware of the extent. Nor did the engine manufacturer realize how much customers valued this aspect of the service. The engine manufacturer therefore adjusted its resource allocation and, as a result, avoided losing a major contract.

This example shows why competitive benchmarking can be less than satisfactory. First, there was no direct dialogue between the engine manufacturers. Hence, any opportunity there might have been for capturing nuances of style and attitude, which play a significant role in cooperative benchmarking, was missed.

Second, the measure used (allocation of engineers to customers) was a finite one and of limited use. A more meaningful measure might have been number of work hours spent by engineers at customer premises or hours allocated to product development compared with hours for firefighting. This might have shown that 30 effective engineers could do the jobs of two or three times the number of less effective ones.

Third, the end result was a one-time improvement against the single measure with no evidence that ongoing improvement could be built in. Yet a benefit of benchmarking is the ongoing opportunities it provides for improvement.

COMPETITIVE ANALYSIS

Sometimes the boundary between good competitive analysis and competitive benchmarking can be a little blurred.

A large, well-known hotel group decided to conduct a competitive benchmarking exercise to help it decide whether or not to move into a new market sector. Accordingly, it sent a team of six employees on a six-month information gathering mission round the country to compare hotels in the target sector.

As well as gathering facts such as quality and number of towels per room, variety and quality of shampoos, bath soaps, and so on, the team tested out the hotels' response times to guest requests (for example, for more coat hangers, new shoelaces), sound insulation between rooms, general friendliness of service, and willingness of staff to help.

At the end of the six-month period, the team submitted its report about potential rivals, strengths and weaknesses, and perceived opportunities. Armed with this information, the hotel group budgeted for a new chain of hotels they felt would beat the competition in every respect, from soap to service to soundproof rooms.

A year after launching, this new chain of hotels had an occupancy rate 10% higher than the rest of the industry.

GPT

There is no single best route into benchmarking. What sets leading companies apart, however, is the determination with which they apply benchmarking for continuous improvement in order to gain and maintain an edge in fiercely competitive markets. Our final snapshot provides an excellent example of this.

GPT Limited was created in 1988 following the merger of the telecommunications businesses of GEC and Plessey. Although both were leaders in the UK and had strong sale in a number of export markets, a global presence was required to compete effectively in the fast-moving telecommunications sector. A major initiative was launched to combine efficiently and effectively the resources of the two companies in order to address this goal and to forge the new corporate culture it required. The subsequent training program involved all of GPT's staff and earned the company a National Training Award.

GPT became jointly owned by GEC (60%) and Siemens (40%) following the takeover of Plessey. The combined telecommunications business of GPT and Siemens and their international experience makes them world leaders.

The strategic change process was continued with part of the program being concentrated on increasing competitive advantage. The two pertinent problems were: how to improve performance and market leadership, and how to develop innovative products and services to enter new markets. One of the techniques that created much interest was competitive benchmarking, so much so that the GPT board decided to launch a specific initiative.

A pilot project covering three major topics was completed in June 1989. The main purpose of this was to investigate the technique and how it could be applied effectively in GPT. One of the learning points was the lack of understanding of the existing problems. It often seemed the deeper one dug, the more elusive the answer became.

However, persistent analysis overcame this hurdle and the results of the pilot were conclusive. Benchmarking was seen as an essential tool for a successful business. Consequently, the GPT board sponsored a second phase of projects to train and develop capability in the technique. Twelve key topics were selected for benchmarking, and a series of seminars was incorporated to facilitate the learning process and share information and contacts.

The second phase was a resounding success. Along the way, the company was voted the best overall performer in a major independent business survey of customer satisfaction. However, while winning awards is satisfying, it is only a way of keeping score. GPT believes that one of the most significant benefits of benchmarking is the acute external focus it develops. The technique is now firmly established to augment the customer focus policy and as an ongoing process in the company's day-to-day activities.

5

AN OVERVIEW OF THE BENCHMARKING PROCESS

NO HIT-AND-MISS PROCESS

REQUIRES AND IMPOSES DISCIPLINE

DEMANDS UNDERSTANDING OF THE BUSINESS

As seen in Chapter 3, effective benchmarking is best approached in the spirit of TQM. The philosophy behind this provides the necessary human elements of empowerment, enthusiasm, and cooperation that effect positive change and help gain commitment to continuous improvement.

Benchmarking is not hit and miss. Nor is it a technique that can be picked up and dropped at whim or according to availability of resources, usually time. There will always be people who look for panaceas and who feel benchmarking may be it. Equally, there will always be those who believe a little of something is better than nothing at all. Approached in this way, it is best left well alone.

Benchmarking is a process. Its overriding characteristic is the discipline it requires and imposes. Rigorously following a logical sequence of steps enables managers to identify what is most important to the business, where improvement is most needed and in which areas; if there is more than one, it would have the most significant impact on performance.

The process encourages, but also demands, intimate understanding of the business before comparisons can be made, gaps identified, or actions implemented. The goal, which is always to achieve competitive superiority, can be realized only over the long term.

As with any process, there are inputs, several of which, as Figure 5.1 shows, are 'soft' or intangible factors, and others that are 'hard' and quantifiable; as well as activities and outputs.

THE INTANGIBLE INPUTS

It is wise to assess, review, or gather the necessary inputs before starting any exercise. In benchmarking the inputs may vary according to the particular process under the microscope, but three of the basic requirements are vision, commitment, and diligence.

Before any major initiative is undertaken, there must be a vision in place of where the organization will be as a result of the initiative. Otherwise, how will people know where they are going or whether they are heading in the right direction? A popular Chinese phrase adopted by David Kearns, president of Xerox Corporation during the first decade of its benchmarking program was: "If we don't change direction we might end up where we're headed."

The fact that a benchmarking program is being considered implies a *desire and a need for change.* However, there is always resistance to change, and it is normally in direct proportion to the degree of change required. This resistance can be overcome by providing the motivation to live with the uncertainty along the journey. If benchmarking is thought of as the vehicle, then vision is the fuel which keeps it going. However, because it is a never-ending journey, the fuel must be something sustainable and renewable.

VISION IS ESSENTIAL FOR CHANGE

The most effective vision should be:

- Inspirational, so that people will be prepared to dedicate extraordinary effort when required; and
- Realizable.

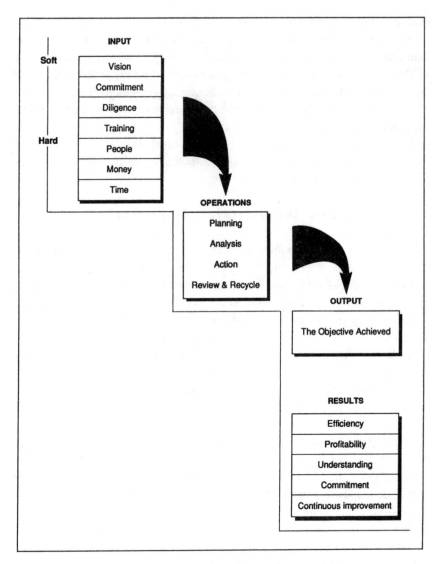

FIGURE 5.1: Benchmarking—the overview

In other words, although vision stems from creativity and lateral thinking and so inhabits some nebulous world, it must be brought down to earth and described with enthusiasm and conviction. And it must include some pointers as to how it can be achieved. Utopian visions are fine for personal dreams but do not translate readily into the harsh realities of the business world. Show people the stepping stones and the chances are they will believe they can walk on water.

It also helps to think of benchmarking as *just one of a number of vehicles* in which to make the journey. People are more likely to come on board if, along with a clear vision of where and why they are going, they understand how the preferred vehicle is going to take them there. No matter how inspirational or idyllic a palm-fringed, peaceful island may be, if the only way to arrive is to paddle 6,000 miles through shark-infested waters in a canoe with no support or defense devices, not many will want to make the effort.

The vision input to benchmarking is the desire to achieve superior status, expressed as "becoming the best." Each person's interpretation is different and there is no single "best." The field is wide open for every company to be the best at something. Real vision implies knowing what the core "something" is for your particular company or organization and how it can be achieved. There are two facets to vision: corporate vision and the benchmarking team vision.

Corporate vision is the overall vision of where the organization is heading and how benchmarking will help make arrival easier. Much of the success of the Xerox and General Electric programs has been attributed to the visions of David Kearns and Jack Welch—the two chief executive officers, respectively—and the vitality with which they shared this. The higher the source of the vision the more zealously it is likely to be followed.

The benchmarking team vision, on the other hand, is very different. Any group involved in a change process encounters resistance and occasional hostility. Individuals within such a group need to share a common vision of where their efforts are leading them to give them the inner strength to overcome negativity. It needs to be clearly stated in words that everyone agrees and understands; otherwise, in the real world, how will anyone know if it has been achieved?

COMMITMENT INCREASES THE SUCCESS RATE

Benchmarking requires considerable time, investment, and effort. The second input therefore is commitment—with a capital "C." The greater this is, the better the chance for achieving results.

The ideal combination is a high level of personal commitment from employees throughout the organization coupled with audible support from as high up the organization as possible. Commitment from employees can be gained by senior management effectively and enthusiastically communicating the vision and voicing their support for benchmarking to achieve this. Time invested in securing this from the outset will speed progress with the benchmarking program.

Inevitably there will be occasions when benchmarking leads to a change of policy, or decisions or investments need senor level sanction. The more critical the area being benchmarked, the higher the level of commitment required to secure support in these areas. If senior executives are on board from the outset, much time is saved between the planning and action phases of the benchmarking process.

It is normal for there to be a long lead time between the start of the benchmarking exercise and achieving the improvements attributable to it. The commitment, therefore, must be more than just verbal.

There are a number of other ways in which it can be expressed, for example:

- The financial support given to the process—a reasonable budget for planning and research, for example;
- Other support resources such as time and facilities available for team meetings, activities, and communications;
- The emotional support available from internal and external sources, either to act as sounding boards during periods of low morale or "expert" help with the technicalities of the benchmarking process;
- The corporate support shown by featuring benchmarking objectives and success stories in house magazine editorials or displaying information across all sites on notice boards;
- Integrating benchmarking objectives into personal appraisal, remuneration, and reward systems.

DILIGENCE MAKES THE TRANSITION POSSIBLE

Benchmarking is a continuous process, with the sequence of steps arranged in logical order. Each requires its own input from the previous one as well as providing the input to the next one. Diligence in following the sequence and in completing each step thoroughly is therefore the third input.

There are several misconceptions about benchmarking. One of these suggests that benchmarking consists of deciding something needs to be improved, making a few visits to perceived "better" companies and then initiating relevant improvements. The mental time frame that accompanies this thinking is on a scale of days or weeks at most. Such visits have been variously dubbed:

- "Industrial Tourism"—people visit other companies just to see what there is to see because it happens to be there.
- "Feel-Good Trips"—people visit other companies, just to see that what other companies do is not as impressive as they had been led to believe and come back feeling good about what they themselves do.
- "Wow! Visits"—the visitor sees companies doing wonderful things and comes away thinking "Wow! If we did that we could be as good as them."

The following dialogue is commonly heard:

A: We ought to install a new accounting/ordering/product launch/telephone system. Which firm shall we visit to benchmark against?

B: What is it you are looking for?

A: We don't know. That's why we want to go and look at what other people are doing.

B: What is wrong with the present system?

A. We don't know if there is anything wrong until we see something better.

B: How will you recognize what is better?

A: We won't know until we see it.

B: What exactly does the present system involve?

A: Well, roughly . . . x, y, and z.

In other words, it is taken for granted that the visit will provide all the questions and all the answers. Not so.

Correctly applied, benchmarking can replace "Wow" with "How." Diligence is what makes the transition possible. It must be applied at every stage of the benchmarking process, but is perhaps most critical at the planning stage. There are good reasons for this:

- Even if the visit may be potentially abortive or fruitless, the team should follow through with the appointment with the host company out of respect.
- It does not help the company's reputation to be seen to be undecided about the information the team is aiming to gather.

- Bear in mind that the people at the host company are also potential customers or PR agents for the company. The team should think of the impression it is creating.
- Support for the team's activities is unlikely to be high if it cannot clearly communicate its objectives and goals.
- If the team has little understanding of what is happening in its own organization, how will it know if another firm is better or worse?

HARD INPUTS ALSO ARE ESSENTIAL

In addition to the combination of soft inputs there are essential hard inputs, for example, people, resources, and training.

- **People.** The people dimension depends on the degree of vision and commitment shown by the chief executive and the senior management team. If managers have support from superiors, they are more likely to give their people's time for benchmarking activities. Similarly, the people will be more dedicated to the process if they are convinced of support and know that their efforts will be rewarded.
- **Resources.** The allocation of financial and physical resource will flow from the soft inputs. Diligence plays a significant role in establishing the credibility to secure resources. Accurate planning of activities will ensure that the optimum resources are requested or allocated to gain the desired results.
- **Training.** Training is an important element, but the best time to feed it into the process depends on a combination of factors. For example: how high is the general awareness level of benchmarking? Are commitment/awareness/skills training necessary? What is being benchmarked? How many people are involved and when? What order of priority/significance is attached? What level of understanding or skill is required?

Problems still can arise even when the senior executives are well versed in the technique, convinced of its efficacy, and committed to its implementation throughout the organization. Responsibility may be devolved to business units but with insufficient or no training, little positive benefit may result.

It is advisable to audit the level of awareness, knowledge, and skills present and required before launching the program. If training is needed, it should take place at appropriate stages.

Remember, benchmarking is not meant to create more work, it is intended to produce more effective work. Training helps in achieving this.

ACTIVITIES IN THE BENCHMARKING PROCESS

With the inputs in place, it is now possible to look at the activities of the process. As detailed in the following chapters, there are four distinct operational stages each comprising the following sequence of steps (see Figure 5.2):

- Stage 1: Planning.
- Stage 2: Analysis.

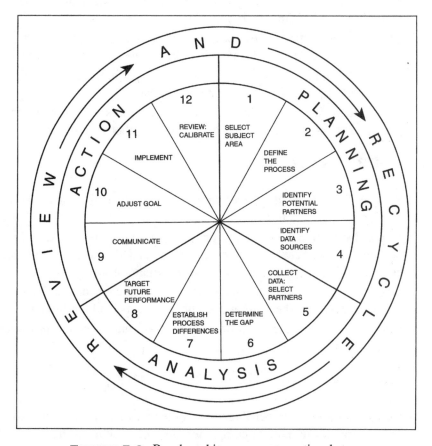

FIGURE 5.2: Benchmarking process operational steps

- Stage 3: Action.
- Stage 4: Review and Recycle.

Each stage must be completed as thoroughly as possible before moving on. In practice, the bulk of time is spent at the planning stage. An 80%/20% split between Planning and Analysis is a good ratio for most benchmarking exercises. Action depends on implementation, so the time involved will vary widely from one exercise to the next. Along with Review and Recycle, Action is ongoing so the measurement of time involved may not be a relevant or accurate guide.

STAGE 1: PLANNING

- Step 1: Select the broad subject area in which to benchmark—manufacturing, warehousing, marketing, etc.
- Step 2: Define the process within that subject area to be benchmarked—e.g., changeover time, picking, or a new product launch.
- Step 3: Preliminarily identify the potential partners against which benchmarking may be possible and beneficial.
- Step 4: Identify the most likely sources of data to substantiate initial perceptions and select the most appropriate method of collection.

STAGE 2: ANALYSIS

- Step 5: Collect the data, and from these confirm the most likely benchmark partners to contact.
- Step 6: Determine the gap between the existing performance and that produced by the benchmark company. Contact and arrange to visit the benchmark company to validate or substantiate information.
- Step 7: Compare the existing process with that at the benchmark company and establish the differences, enhancements, and modifications.
- Step 8: Target future performance to take into account process improvements.

STAGE 3: ACTION

- Step 9: Communicate benchmarking objectives and results throughout the organization, other companies, and the benchmarking partner where possible and relevant.

- Step 10: Adjust goals in light of desired performance improvements stimulated by comparison with the benchmark partner; develop corrective improvement plans to achieve these.
- Step 11: Implement and monitor the corrective improvement plans.
- Step 12: Review progress and calibrate performance improvements and targets.

STAGE 4: REVIEW AND RECYCLE

Although shown as the fourth stage, this nevertheless has two guises. It is the last of the 12 sequential steps in the process of benchmarking, but it also interweaves at various points throughout the Planning, Analysis, and Action stages.

For example, collecting data and selecting benchmark partners (Step 5) may bring forth information previously not available to help identify potential benchmarking partners (Step 3), which necessitates a Review of the partners previously listed.

Similarly, determining the gap (Step 6) in the light of detailed information from the benchmark partner may not be possible without more work on the in-house process definition, resulting in the need to more exactly define the process (Step 2).

Because it is difficult to know in advance how much reviewing and recycling will be appropriate, the main point is to allow contingency time when planning the benchmarking exercise. Without this there is a danger that the team feel pressured to report back by a fixed date with unprofessional or incomplete recommendations.

OUTPUTS CAN BE DIFFICULT TO MEASURE

"Output" is frequently confused with "Result." A quick rule of thumb is that an output is always measurable, (e.g., weekly production per machine, current delivered by a circuit, or information produced by a computer) or visible (a machine/carton of milk/sheet of steel). A result, on the other hand, may be either quantitative or qualitative (the score of a sporting contest or the consequence of an action).

Translated into benchmarking, the output should reflect the measurable achievement of the objective of the exercise. This may be directly quantifiable in terms of "cut machine down-time back by 75%." Alternatively, it may be measurable from indicators, such as "customer satisfaction increases":

- Repeat orders up by X%;
- Order size increased by Y%;
- Incomplete orders down by Z%;

Whenever the output is uncertain, or not directly measurable, the shortcut is to ask "which indicators reflect this output?" and then assign measures to those indicators. If indicators cannot readily be identified, then possibly the process is not correctly understood or has not been accurately mapped.

Outputs are considered often to be most difficult to measure in the service sector. Service, however, is always the result of the process that delivers it. Where a process exists, output indicators can always be found and measured.

RESULTS MAY BE DIFFICULT TO ISOLATE

Benchmarking is an ongoing process that eventually melds to become another facet of corporate culture. Although results are difficult to isolate, some cited by practicing companies include:

- **Greater efficiency.** This is an almost inevitable result of analyzing, understanding, and "tidying up" existing processes even without benchmarking. When comparisons are made with similar processes elsewhere, further efficiencies result.

  Good benchmarking companies make it a habit to assess and improve the process while helping and training people to work to the best of their ability. This ratchets up the efficiency of the operations still further.

- **Improved understanding.** Involving people in benchmarking results in improved appreciation across the broad spectrum of a company's activities on a number of different levels.

  First, because teams from across the organization are involved, each member gains understanding of operations from different perspectives. The longer that benchmarking continues, the more people learn to respect and understand the importance of other players in the team and the organization.

Second, since it is impossible to benchmark effectively without thorough knowledge of the systems and processes, increased understanding of how and why these interact is gained.

Third, good benchmarking relies on effective corporate goals and missions. This means that corporate leaders are required to think through and communicate these clearly; and employees gain greater insight than might be the case without a benchmarking program.

- **Heightened commitment.** This results from a combination of greater efficiency and understanding plus the engagement of all people in the organization. Whenever involvement is encouraged, self-respect grows and greater commitment results.

As the Chinese proverb says:

Tell me, I may hear.
Show me, I may remember.
Involve me, I will understand.

- **Continuous improvement.** This is the prime justification for benchmarking. Some people worry whether continuous improvement or superiority can be maintained if every company is benchmarking against the best. However, not all managers who see best practice find the means to implement it in their own organization. Also, the goalposts are movable. There will always be innovators, technology will always improve, and some people will always strive to improve beyond the best that currently exists.

- **Increased profitability.** Improving operating efficiency to become more competitive is one of the prime motivators for benchmarking programs. It is difficult to assess in hard financial terms with complete accuracy how much of an increase stems from a particular initiative. There is, however, consensus among practicing companies that benchmarking is an extremely powerful tool. It highlights duplications, dysfunctions, anomalies, and bad practices enabling these to be removed and replaced by better practice. This results in increased efficiency, lower cost, improved cash flow, and better profitability.

6

THE PLANNING STAGE: PROCESSES

MASTER THE BASICS

SYSTEMATIC APPROACH IS NECESSARY

COMPLETE EACH PROCESS STEP

There is no need to invest large sums of money in a luxury car in order to learn to drive. The ability to accelerate from 0–60 miles per hour in under six seconds is uninspiring when the learner is still trying to master the rudiments of start, go, and stop. The same rule applies with implementing benchmarking. It is not necessary to begin with a model exercise that is the envy of everyone and will be watched and monitored with anxious interest. It is better to master the basics in an everyday "test-bed" or "trial run" situation that does not arouse too much attention elsewhere in the organization but could make a sufficiently noticeable improvement to convert some of the inevitable skeptics.

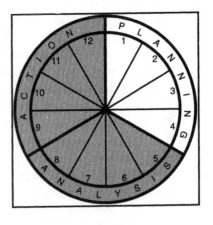

In such situations, it may be less important to consider each step in detail than to find out how the overall model works and gain a degree of confidence in the approach. However, once the basics have been mastered, a more systematic sophisticated approach enhances performance across a variety of situations. The more crucial the need for improvement, the more important it becomes to pay rigorous attention to completing each step of the process.

The first four steps making up the planning phase are the most time-intensive of any benchmarking exercise. Experience has proved repeatedly, however, that the quality of results achieved is directly related to the effort invested at the outset. In this chapter, we discuss the first two of these that concern the selection of processes.

STEP 1: SELECTING THE SUBJECT AREA TO BENCHMARK

Companies adopting the "trial runs" approach to benchmarking tend to choose the subject area as the result of another initiative. For example, it may be selected as a result of a problem-solving exercise or come to light through a customer survey. Topics with an immediate impact, such as delivery scheduling, complaints, and telephone handling, could fall into this category. Solutions tend to be reactive, the priority being on implementation in the shortest possible time to effect a result. Benchmarking makes a valuable contribution in these situations, but such shortfalls may be dealt with by standard problem-solving (or similar) mechanisms.

In major benchmarking projects, however, the starting point is identification of a subject area within which improvement is critical. It is a focused approach. It is not a case of throwing a bunch of ideas into a hat, pulling one out and going to work on that, or on one person's pet subject.

The criteria for selecting the subject area are:

- It should be of strategic importance to the business;
- Improvement in that area will make a significant contribution to overall business results.

It is important at this early stage to paint on a large canvas. The obvious ideas are not necessarily the best ones. People cannot help becoming involved in their own speciality to the exclusion of wider business concerns. The possibility of tunnel vision should be acknowledged and the opportunity taken to generate a wide variety of ideas. Tools such as brainstorming are effective for this purpose. Outside "experts" may help if the organization has difficulty focusing on external as well as internal factors.

Answering the following questions may help with identification and clarification.

- *Which business are we in?* This may be obvious, but beware of taking it too much at face value.

This question does not generate the answer to "What to benchmark?" It is, however, a basic question to address in any strategy formulation exercise. For example, when television became available to a mass market in the 1950s, Hollywood producers, who thought they were in the business of making films, felt threatened. They saw their market decline as more people stayed in to watch television and fewer went out to see movies. Had they realized they were in the business of popular entertainment rather than making big screen movies they might have cooperated with television producers instead of trying to compete against them. Their market could have grown phenomenally instead of declining.

- *What must we do to remain in business?* This means the core activity(ies) that keep the firm in business.

Basic survival factors, such as operating within the law and paying bills, are not included here. It is assumed these are a given to any operating business.

- *What must we do to be really successful in our business?* These are factors that distinguish leaders from followers.

The answer is not simply "Make X% profit" or a variation on that theme. It is the activities in which the business has to excel to generate the returns that satisfy the business's success criteria. As such, there may be several answers.

- *Which single factor would make the most significant improvement to our customer/supplier/employee relationships?* In answering this question, both internal and external customers/suppliers should be considered. The quality of internal relationships has a distinct impact on external ones.

This question should provoke creative thoughts. It is not sufficient to consider the world as it is; imagine what it will be like in, say five or 10 years and then ask what would significantly improve relationships. The aim is to generate ideas without constraints imposed by current, short term/economics or politics. The list can be analyzed later to identify and prioritize key improvements.

- *Which areas, if improved, would make the most significant contribution to our bottom line results?* No business can afford to ignore this question, but it should be a qualifying rather than a primary question to address.

If placed higher up the order, there is a danger this factor may dominate, causing other answers to be framed only in financial terms. This may overshadow creative thinking and restrict possibilities for improvement.

Brainstorming is one method of generating a number of ideas for possible subject areas. The first two questions establish the canvas while the remainder direct the focus. The following box illustrates a typical question-and-answer sequence for a videotape manufacturer.

Question 1: Which business are we in?
  Home entertainment
Question 2: What must we do to remain in business?
  Obtain rights to films.
  Efficiently produce video copies.
  Market effectively.
  Distribute in a timely manner.
Question 3: What must we do to be really successful in our business?
  Be the best supplier of most popular videos.
Question 4: Which single factor would make the most signifcant improvement to our customer/supplier/employee relationships?
  Faster delivery on demand to customers.
Question 5: Which areas, if improved, would make the most significant contribution to our bottom line?
  Increased market share as a result of more effective distribution.

The objective is to establish a maximum of three subject areas in which benchmarking would make a considerable impact. These are then prioritized. It is wise to direct attention to a small number of areas, particularly in the early stages of benchmarking when knowledge of the technique needs to be developed alongside the process itself. It will prove difficult otherwise to prioritize key processes to benchmark.

The question to bear in mind is: *Is this what is **really** important?* Difficulty in agreeing could signal too narrow a focus. The strategic overview—imagine taking an aerial photo of the business—should extend from suppliers through employees to end-users.

Worksheets 1 and 2 help focus on subject areas. They can be found in the Appendix.

SUPPLY CHAIN

Selection of the subject area may be influenced by the company's, or function's, position in the supply chain. This is the complete string of events leading up to delivery of the product or service to the end-user. Although it is likely to play a less significant role in "trial runs" than when benchmarking is drawn into the strategic armory, identification of the supply chain is an important element in gaining an overview.

For example, in many manufacturing companies, costs associated with suppliers account for as much as 50% of the total cost of goods. Additionally, for those components or sub-assemblies a company makes for itself, more efficient external sources may be available. Identifying and taking advantage of these could increase the number of supplier contacts and, consequently, their influence on cost of goods.

SUPPLY MANAGEMENT: HOW EFFICIENT IS IT?

- What is the total number of suppliers the company deals with?
- Are there secondary or back-up suppliers?
- How competitive are the company's suppliers in the world market?
- How well are they managed by the company?
- How are supplier quality assurance or evaluation managed?
- How effective is the management of cross-functional processes that promote good supply management, such as strategic make versus buy analyses?

Any company, or function, that depends on suppliers for half or more of the total cost of goods could find that supply management is a more important subject area in which to benchmark than say, production, distribution, or customer service. The closer to the beginning of the chain that improvements can be identified, the less waste is built-in or carried forward to subsequent stages. The inefficiency multiplier effect is thus reduced. Superior handling of functional and cross-functional supply management processes may have greater impact on profitability and competitive position than, say, speeding up new product launches or improving sales planning.

The real value of focusing on the supply chain lies in:

• Identifying suppliers in the correct sequence;
• Considering the critical inputs to each stage of the business;
• Recognizing the extent of their influence on the business.

Drawing a model of the business supply chain helps clarify thinking. Seeing the overall picture also makes the detail easier to absorb. However, not all real-life examples will be as straightforward as the simple model shown in Figure 6.1.

Worksheet 3 for drawing up a supply chain model can be found in the Appendix.

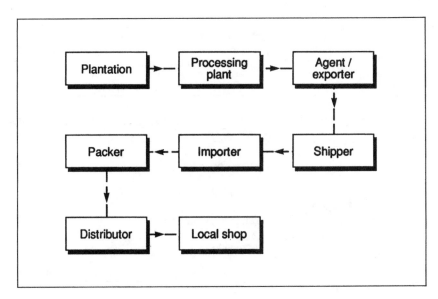

FIGURE 6.1: Tea supply chain model

STEP 2: DEFINE THE PROCESS TO BENCHMARK

Having identified the subject area in which to focus attention, the next stage is to select the precise process central to the entire exercise.

Process definition is one of the most critical steps in a benchmarking exercise. In fact, because much of benchmarking is comparing processes, it is difficult to complete some of the subsequent steps without spending sufficient time analyzing, questioning, rationalizing, and validating this. There are no "quick" ways to do this. In any mature organization, processes will be numerous, complex, and linked by an intricate and often tangled web.

As with any complex exercise, the best place to start is at the beginning and proceed in a logical fashion. Visualize a large Spanish onion as in Figure 6.2. The outer skin of the onion represents the subject areas, which are usually the overall executive management processes within the organization. These can also be referred to as prime, or Level 1 processes.

Peel away this outer skin from the onion and a second skin is revealed, as shown in Figure 6.3. This represents Level 2 processes; those directly

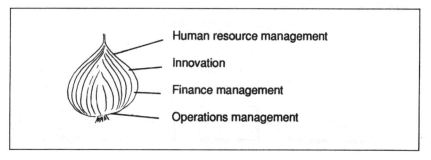

Human resource management

Innovation

Finance management

Operations management

FIGURE 6.2: Every organization has layers of processes

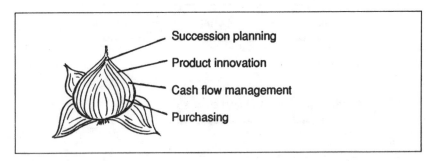

Succession planning

Product innovation

Cash flow management

Purchasing

FIGURE 6.3: Stripping away the outer layers reveals another layer

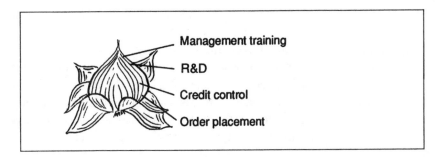

Management training

R&D

Credit control

Order placement

FIGURE 6.4: Further peeling exposes another level

responsible for supporting the overall executive management processes at Level 1.

Strip away this onion skin and yet another is revealed below. This represents the Level 3 processes, which support those at Level 2 as shown in Figure 6.4.

Just like an onion has successive layers of "skin" right down to the heart, every organization has numerous layers of processes. It is not possible to see the next skin of the onion until the outer covering has been removed. Similarly, it is often not possible to identify the precise process to benchmark until many others have been peeled away.

Worksheet 4 for peeling the onion can be found in the Appendix.

Royal Mail, for example, originally selected telemarketing as a process to benchmark. When the components of this were analyzed, it was found the critical areas were: answering the phone and ending the call. Consequently, these two sub-processes were each investigated rather than the encompassing process of telemarketing.

It is this degree of detailed attention that is required to identify the critical process. This plays a crucial role later when selecting the benchmark. For example, a problem for a retail bank was channeling customers, already waiting in the banking hall to be served, to the service counter smoothly and quickly. This generated a host of ideas about where to look for benchmarks, including fast-food and other service-centered organizations.

The ultimate goal is to identify, analyze, and describe individual processes, indicating where each links into the next and who is responsible for it. A suitable analogy is completing a jigsaw puzzle. Starting with a mass of separate pieces (processes), they are gradually joined together to create a picture that resembles an organizational chart with processes instead of jobs in the boxes. Each is given a number that indicates its position in the hierarchy and builds up to a process map (see page 66 for a process map).

The number will depend on the complexity of the business and maturity of the organization. Xerox Corporation in the US, for example, has identified 10 Level 1 processes with a total of 57 Level 2 processes—and these are just from the factory gate outwards. Examples at Level 1 include order fulfillment, information technology management, and business management. Included at Level 2 (under order fulfilment) are:

- Order processing.
- Customer service.
- Product production.

Under information technology management:

- Systems development.
- Production systems support.
- Business systems management and coordination.

Under business management:

- Business strategy development.
- Business planning.
- Business process and operations management.

These lists form just a sample of the Level 2 inclusions. "Business process and operations management" is further broken down into five more processes, including:

- Process specification.
- Benchmarking.

Both of these can be further broken down into component sub-processes.

DESIGNATING PROCESS REFERENCE NUMBERS

In the case of Xerox Corporation, a process within benchmarking would be numbered 8.3.4x where:

8. = The prime Level 1 process reference
    (i.e. Business management, which is eighth of the 10 Level 1
    processes)
.3 = Number of the Level 2 process
    (i.e. Business process and operations management)
.4 = Number of the Level 3 process
    (i.e. Benchmarking)
x = Ranking of the Level 4 process
    (e.g. Process definition)

This numeric "ranking" continues until no further associated sub-processes can be identified.

With so many processes potentially available to select for benchmarking, it is clear they must be analyzed and their ranking and importance to the business prioritized. The more "strategic" benchmarking becomes to the organization, the more relevant this is.

Although time consuming, it becomes less so with familiarity and as the activity permeates through the company. Ideally it should be done by individuals and work groups identifying and writing up their own work processes, showing how they interlink. With the support of teams such as focus groups, quality circles, or project networks, gradually these can be drawn together and linked into the total "picture" over a reasonable period of time.

Work practices develop through custom and habit, many continuing long beyond their useful life. In the general run of business, these are not questioned. However, it is often because of cumbersome or superfluous practices that jobs are complex or take longer than necessary. Pursuing simple questions like "What/how/why do I/you do . . . something?" can highlight and gradually lead to stripping out much that is unnecessary or unproductive effort. Jobs become more efficient, costs are cut, often by a surprising amount, and because nobody likes wasting time, people feel their efforts are better directed and more rewarding. Over the long term a willing attitude develops, efficiencies increase, and business prospers as a result.

Analyzing and understanding the process, its component parts, and relationships in the total system are crucial to the success of a benchmarking exercise. The analysis has four aspects:

- Definition;
- Boundaries;
- Steps;
- Mapping.

DEFINITION

Most of us know what we mean when we describe something we are involved in. Much of the time when we talk with others we make the subconscious assumption that they share the same mental picture. If it is something that they are to become involved in, this frequently leads to misinterpretation and confusion. However, it is only when things go wrong that the misunderstandings surface; what was obvious to one party was clear as mud to the other.

This highlights the need for accurate description. Never assume people "see" things just as you do. Try the following exercise with someone you know fairly well. Describe a dream you have had recently with as much detail as you can. Ask your listener to replay the dream to you describing how he or she "sees" the surroundings/colors/scenery. Do these bear any resemblance to what you saw in your dream?

The process to be analyzed is the one that delivers the output requiring improvement. Unless this output has been accurately defined, it may prove difficult to measure or identify the process that delivers it. "Customer Service," for example, could be the "on-time, in-full, delivery service provided to national account customers in the home market" or it might be "answering all external telephone calls within four rings." Knowing precisely what each output word means is vital.

Everyone understands a specific process from the perspective of how it relates to their work. This is subjective and personal. In describing it so that others may be able to understand, every detail must be included, no matter how trivial or irrelevant it may seem, thus leaving little room for ambivalence or misunderstanding.

OUTPUT DEFINITION

If customer service is to be improved effectively, several aspects must be defined:

Customer: Who is this?

Internal/external? National account? Top 10%/all? Home/overseas? Distributor/end-user?

Service: What/where?

What? Response to telephone/technical support/complaints resolution/after-sales?

Where? Customer premises/overseas/reception hall?

BOUNDARIES

When asked to describe how to make a cup of coffee, cook a meal, or arrange a vacation, certain initial questions require answers: "Regular or decaffeinated?" Roast beef or chicken?" Deciding where to go or contacting a travel agent?"

Similarly, process start and cut-off points need to be established before moving to the next stages of analysis.

PROCESS BOUNDARIES

What is the output of the process?
• Order fitted, complaint handled, delivery made.
• May be more than one; if so, check if really the same process.

Who is the customer?
• The recipient of the output.

What are the customer's requirements?
• How, what, when, where, why?

Is this what your process delivers?
• Can it be improved?
• If not, is it the right process?

What are the start and end points?
• Delivery—from factory gate to shipper?

Who owns the process?
• Name the person responsible for improvement and with control over resources.

Boundaries must be described precisely and clearly because they are often the root of problems or dysfunctions. The more interfaces or junction points there are, the greater the potential for delay and failure.

The need to define boundaries flags up whether, and how far, they extend beyond the individual, or group, responsibility (for example, where they involve more than one department or function). Where this happens, relevant others should be identified and involved.

When the boundaries have been established, a named process owner should be allocated. This is someone with responsibility and control over the resources. It is preferable if he or she is directly involved in the process. Longer term, the owner is responsible for reviewing and monitoring best practices and ensuring that improvements continue to be made.

PROCESS STEPS

Having agreed on the process definition and boundaries, the next stage is to list the steps involved in the correct sequence. This means documenting what happens "on the ground," not what is written in the manual.

Few processes are the concern of a single individual. This stage should therefore include the views of anyone with an input to, or output from, the process. Depending on the point at which they interact with it, individuals will have different ideas about what happens, when, and by whom. All of these must be taken into account.

One way of dealing with the variety of views is to write the individual steps on "Post-It" type notes and then collect them together either on a board or table. When everyone is sure all the steps have been identified, they can be sorted, arranged in the correct sequence, and the list created. Certainly, throughout the benchmarking process the most frequently heard phrase should be: "Hey! What do we/you/they actually mean by that?" Moreover, this exercise may have to be repeated several times before the process is fully understood and everyone is satisfied that the final list is an accurate representation.

Worksheet 5, which lists process steps, can be found in the Appendix.

The process steps chart (Figure 6.5) has a column headed "Measurement notes." It is important that this be completed as fully as possible.

SPEED = SIMPLICITY

When they analyzed Inquiry Response Time with regard to the customer order handling process, Lucas Aerospace Ltd. discovered that up to 20 ownership changes (e.g. release notes, export/import documentation, credit control, sales ledger) could be involved. Changes resulting from benchmarking this procedure reduced these to three. The consequent time taken to "process" orders decreased from an average of 30 to six days (the response time requested by customers).

Even for the most simple procedure, ascribing accurate quantitative figures leads to clarity of current performance and targets. If undertaken from the outset, improvements are easier to record over time.

For some processes, such as those requiring the movement of documents or objects around the organization, it may be helpful at this point to draw a "flow" diagram. This is particularly useful for operations that

Process name:		
Charted by:		
Date:		
Details of method process steps	**Type of activity**	**Measurement notes**
1.	....	....
2.	....	....
3.	....	....
4.	....	....
5.	....	....
6.	....	....
7.	....	....
8.	....	....
9.	....	....
10.	....	....
11.	....	....
12.	....	....
13.	....	....
14.	....	....
15.	....	....
16.	....	....

FIGURE 6.5: Typical process steps

involve a single item (an application or order form, for example) being handled by a number of people. At a glance it will be seen whether the item frequently crosses an office, department, or site boundary. Significant delays and backtracking, for instance, are immediately visible.

Conventional symbols indicate which steps involve any of five "activities" (see Figure 6.6). This picture can provide a starting point for initial improvement opportunities.

The example in Figure 6.7 lists the steps involved in making a cup of instant coffee and the resultant flow diagram is shown in Figure 6.8. This simplified example shows a straightforward flow. Swings toward frequent

○	Operation	The main "activities" in a process
⇓	Transport	Movement of people, materials, paper, information, etc.
D	Delay	Temporary storage, delay or hold-up between consecutive activities
☐	Inspection	Indicates a check-point (quality or quantity)
▽	Storage	Deliberate storage, such as filing.

FIGURE 6.6: Conventional process flow symbols

delay or inspection signal overdependence on control and check mechanisms. These create frustration and time wasting and inevitably result in customer dissatisfaction.

PROCESS MAPPING

This is the final step in defining the process. The map gives an easily assimilated overview allowing the relationships, interfaces and potential failure points to be visible immediately—a significant factor when comparisons are later made with processes elsewhere. As with listing the sequential steps, the discipline involved in drawing the map prompts constant questioning and validation. Duplications and potential failure points

Process name: making a cup of instant coffee

Details of method process steps	Type of activity	Measurement notes
1. Fill Mug	operation	1 cup
2. Boil water in microwave	op / delay	3 minutes
3. Find jar in pantry	op / delay	
4. Check jar contains coffee	inspection	
5. Move jar to counter	operation	
6. Fetch teaspoon	operation	
7. Open jar	operation	
8. Retrieve Mug from Microwave	operation	
9. Put coffee in Mug	operation	1 spoonful
10. Stir	operation	
11.		
12.		
13.		
14.		
15.		
16.		

FIGURE 6.7: Typical process steps

are clearly illustrated, and these can be eliminated frequently by common-sense suggestions. The resultant costs savings are often substantial.

It can be a salutory experience to map a process. The less direct the association with it, or the smaller the input, the more potentially bewildering the map. Time and again the process map proves how few people really understand the process. As with listing the steps, it is probably impossible for one person to produce a complete map. Everyone involved should be given the

PROCESS STEPS

1. Fill mug
2. Boil water in microwave
3. Find jar in pantry
4. Check it contains coffee
5. Move jar to counter
6. Fetch Teaspoon
7. Open jar
8. Retrieve mug from microwave
9. Put coffee in cup
10. Stir
11. Coffee ready

FIGURE 6.8: Flow diagram for making instant coffee

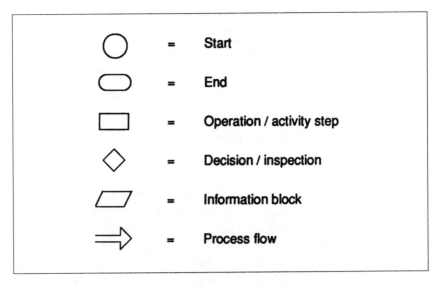

FIGURE 6.9: Conventional process mapping symbols

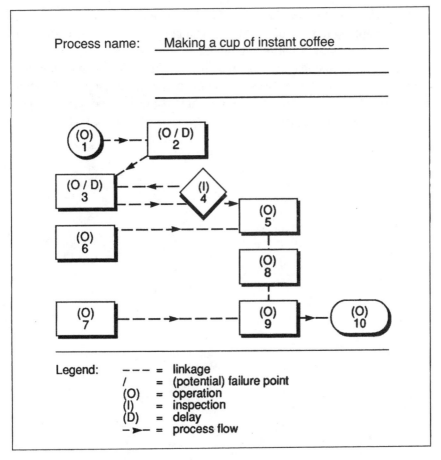

Process name: Making a cup of instant coffee

Legend: - - - = linkage
            /   = (potential) failure point
            (O)   = operation
            (I)   = inspection
            (D)   = delay
            - ►- = process flow

FIGURE 6.10: Process map for making a cup of instant coffee

opportunity to contribute. This exercise provides excellent training for the teamwork necessary to facilitate subsequent improvements.

Mapping is a particularly effective way of describing complex processes. Written descriptions could run to many pages that, apart from being time consuming and tedious to read before comprehending every detail, are susceptible to misinterpretation. Later in the benchmarking exercise, when processes are compared with better practices elsewhere, documentation would be extremely cumbersome. Mapping provides a comprehensive and comprehensible means of comparison between the current and desired process and one where relevant improvements can readily be seen by everyone.

As with the flow diagrams, universally recognized symbols exist for process mapping to provide a "common language" that will be understood across departmental or national boundaries (see Figure 6.9).

The simple coffee making example given in Figure 6.10 is shown in map form. Not many work processes will be so compact. Complete walls, sometimes even rooms, may be needed for a single map with tapes connecting to outlines of interrelated processes or enlargements of specific sections.

7

THE PLANNING STAGE: PARTNERS

**CONTRASTS WITH COMPETITIVE ANALYSIS
REQUIRES MULTISKILLED GROUPS AND
LATERAL THINKING AND DATA GATHERING**

The previous chapter examined the first two steps of the planning stage. Equally important are the two steps discussed in this chapter that lead to the eventual choice of partner. The word "partner" is used throughout benchmarking and reflects its cooperative emphasis. This collaborative partnership concept is a contrast with competitive analyses that can be conducted without contact with, or agreement from, other companies.

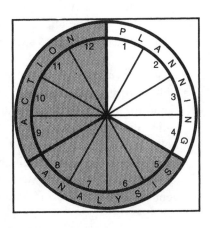

STEP 3: IDENTIFY POTENTIAL BENCHMARKING PARTNERS

The following two questions provide the starting point in the search for suitable partners:

WHO IS BEST?

Following is a list of some responses given by a multinational gathering of senior managers when asked which organization they thought was the best at employing and retaining good people:

The Armed Forced
Airline companies
The Secret Service
Hewlett Packard
Disney

- Who/what is better (at the particular process) than us?
- To whom is this process key for survival?

There are no instant answers or world directories of best practice, but a combination of lateral thinking and organized data gathering will produce a number of options.

Assembling a multiskill, cross-functional group to brainstorm generates more creative ideas than specialist groups. All suggestions are valid at this stage. Questions should be reserved for the end of the exercise.

At the end of the brainstorming session certain qualifying criteria must be decided to validate and shorten the list of ideas. These will fall into a number of broad categories such as:

- Language (national and "corporate").
- Culture (organizational and national)—it may, for instance, prove difficult for a private enterprise to make significant progress with a nationalized one.
- Politics (internal, local, or national).
- Location (in the example given in the box, the question was posed by an American and the answer sought was Federal Express. However, the venue was in the UK and nobody came up with this suggestion).
- Ethics.
- Environmental factors.

When all these have been considered, the question to answer is: Where can we look for compatible, cooperative, and accessible partners? Much will depend on the process chosen to benchmark. Essentially, however, there are three locations where the answer might be found:

- Internally;
- Externally;
- Global best practice.

Internal partners may be found in the same business and at the same or other location. This would be particularly apt if the process under the microscope were, say, telephone answering, complaints handling, or document processing, which are dealt with across the organization or at a variety of points. External partners may be located in other businesses (or countries) within the same group (such as warehousing), or from other companies within the same industry (for a non-competing process such as health and safety). Best practice partners are selected regardless of business, industry sector, or geographical location. The overriding factor is

TABLE 7.1

LOCATING BENCHMARKING PARTNERS

INTERNAL	EXTERNAL	BEST PRACTICE
Functions/departments/ at same or other location of same business/company.	Other business within same group/ or other company in same industry.	Any company, sector or location.
Advantages Same language, culture systems. Ease of access to data. Existing communication channels. Low threat. Good test bed for technique. Relatively quick pay-back possible.	**Advantages** Similar structure/ constraints. If same group, ease of access to data. Relatively low threat if in same group.	**Advantages** May lead to signif-icant improvement. Possible high returns. May uncover break-throughs. Significantly broadens corporate outlook.
Drawbacks Could inhibit external focus. May only give adequate returns. May foster complacency.	**Drawbacks** Legal/ethical considerations. Potential partners may not know/ understand approach. Relatively long-term horizon required.	**Drawbacks** Relatively difficult to gather data. Long-term horizon necessary. "Best" can be controversial.

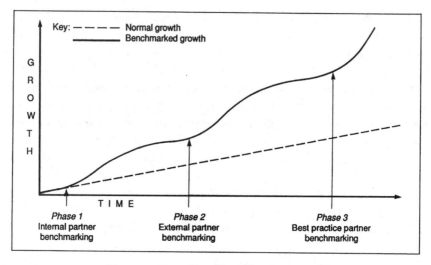

FIGURE 7.1: Benchmarking for growth

that they have established best practice in the process under consideration (see Table 7.1).

The learning curve in benchmarking develops from internal, through external, to best practice (see Figure 7.1).

INTERNAL PARTNERS

Most organizations start with internal comparisons wherever possible. This makes a great deal of sense, because there are relatively few hurdles to overcome in terms of language, culture, and data availability/accessibility. Hierarchies are understood and communication channels generally exist that make it relatively straightforward to visit or telephone someone. Depending on how far down the quality path the company is, many of the features of benchmarking will be familiar from other improvement or problem-solving processes (focus groups and statistical process control, for example).

Benchmarking internally provides a useful nursery slope. Within reason, any question is allowable or forgivable. Far better to learn on safe territory than a strange field. Theories, ideas, and techniques can be tested and honed before subjecting them to outside challenges. Teams can develop familiarity with their own work process before going outside and seeing what others are doing. This is essential if potential for improvement is to be recognized.

Internal benchmarking can be rewarding and produce some relatively quick returns. However, it should not remain the sole form of benchmarking over an extended period. This could have negative consequences, even to the extent of rejuvenating some of the problems originally eliminated—complacency, tunnel vision, and arrogance, for example.

It is crucial to maintain a balance between internal improvement and external best practice for the organization to benefit over the long term.

EXTERNAL PARTNERS

Eventually there comes a point where it is either no longer possible or desirable to improve against internal performance, or major changes (unlikely to be stimulated internally) are needed. Although external comparisons may seem more threatening, they have a higher probability of producing significant returns, discovering innovations, or exploding paradigms. There is a general perception that improvements to existing processes may take longer to identify and implement if external comparisons are sought. This may be true, but a single alteration or adaptation based on practice noted elsewhere could spark an innovation that revolutionizes the way an operation is carried out in your own company.

The constant focus on processes gives a far wider choice of potential partners, making it easy to avoid direct product competitors. Even in rare cases where competitors are willing to cooperate, this involves the risk of industry myopia. The search is for an innovation that will give an edge over direct competitors and not one that merely makes everyone in the industry equally good. More significant, perhaps, is that competitor benchmarking may be perceived in the "outside world" as collusion.

EFFECTIVE COMPETITOR BENCHMARKING

National steel markets traditionally tend to be exclusive, one reason being that steel is expensive to ship over long distances.

In seeking to improve its customer service processes, British Steel benchmarked itself against Nippon Steel in Japan. The particular focus was on Nissan Japan, to which Nippon Steel is the number one supplier. The lessons learned from this exercise helped substantially to improve British Steel's reputation with Nissan Motor Manufacturing UK.

Nonetheless, there are instances where competitor benchmarking is beneficial. Processes that relate to health and safety or environmental protection and are for the general good of the global community fall into this category. Additionally, there are occasions when competitors compete in terms of product but in totally exclusive markets. Nationalized industries or those involving highly perishable products could be included here.

In every external exercise, it is advisable to draw up a framework at the outset detailing the basis for proceeding. This wise precaution reduces the risk of any misunderstanding or ambiguity. The agreement should include areas/questions not open to discussion or comparison and should be sensitive to each organization's perception of its particular competitive edge. Guidelines exist for agreements between direct competitors that detail specific exclusions such as price, markets, size, share of markets, etc. In most cases, strict time limits will be attached to the exercise to avoid suspicion of collusion.

BEST PRACTICE PARTNERS

All benchmarking is ultimately geared to implementing innovations and improvements based on best practice. However, finding best practice can involve a long search, and comparisons may be unrealistic if the gap is extraordinarily wide. What happens in effect, therefore, is that throughout internal and external benchmarking, the search is always for measurably better practice. This provides yardsticks and milestones against which to target improvement, but with the clear understanding that each is a successive step on the journey toward the best.

There is rarely a fixed point at which an organization makes the decision find and then compare itself against the best. Much will depend on its performance record, how favorable this was at the outset, and how much has since been improved. There are no hard and fast rules or guidelines that set down the point at which external benchmarking is finished and best practice begins. It is usually a gradual progression from better to best, the latter often only recognizable with the benefit of hindsight.

It is best practice comparisons that potentially spark improvements providing the most significant rewards and financial returns. The first question to resolve, however, is "What is Best?" The best car, for example, could be the fastest, cheapest, largest, most secure or adaptable, and so on, depending on the selection criteria set. When looking for best practice processes, it is vital to be absolutely clear about the definition of what this means for the business before beginning the search. If the

SMOOTH OPERATORS

As part of its TQM program, Remington Arms, a subsidiary of DuPont, conducted a customer survey. One of the "customer needs" that ranked highly was smoother, shinier ammunition shells.

Remington treated this seriously. Its problem was how to satisfy this need. Where could a heavy industrial manufacturer look for a process that produced smooth, polished ammunition shells? It took a long time and much lateral thought before the solution was found.

The industry sector eventually selected was cosmetics, where smooth, shiny casings are produced for lipsticks. A partnership was established with Revlon, and benchmarking against its practices enabled Remington Arms to make the required improvement to its ammunition shells.

search is for the best widget drilling process, first define the widget, and then define drilling.

The feature that most clearly distinguishes best practice benchmarking is the creativity applied to the search for a partner. The most radical improvement ideas come from areas most would never think to look at, yet when found everyone says: "Hey, why didn't I/we/you think of that?"

The broader the horizon, the greater the likelihood that an entirely new perspective will be found. How about Undertakers for customer care, or Fashion Designers for innovations, or Primary Schools for simplicity? Nor should the search be limited to the corporate world. The Apple Macintosh computer was designed after watching the way children, not managers, learn.

When selecting potential partners:

- The partner should be measurably better.
- The partner may be found within your business at same location, in other locations but same business, different businesses but same in company/group; different companies but same industry, or completely outside the industry.

- Where possible, avoid direct competitors, unless markets are exclusive or processes are general and affect the whole industry.
- With any partner, be aware of legal or ethical considerations, and draw up a procedure agreement at an early stage.
- When seeking "best" practice, define clearly what is understood by "best" for your company or organization.

Worksheet 6 for selecting partners can be found in the Appendix.

STEP 4: IDENTIFY DATA SOURCES AND SELECT APPROPRIATE METHOD OF COLLECTION

Data collection is a vital part of the benchmarking process. In particular, detailed planning is essential to ensure that attention is directed at the areas most likely to generate suitable information. The emphasis is on practicability, not academic research.

If objectives are correctly and accurately defined, there is less likelihood of diversions or wasted resource. The world is full of data. It is easy to become inundated with data; the skill lies in knowing what is needed and in collecting the right, i.e. useful, information.

Before assigning tasks, therefore, it is useful to consider the answers to the following, which will provide a working framework:

- What is the *objective*?
- What do we *need* to look for and *why?*
- How *accurate* must the data be?
- How *much* information do we need?
- How *much* time and resource can we allocate to data collection—people, budgets, and so on?

Responding to such questions might establish, for example, that:

- A maximum of three potential partners is necessary for comparison. Annual performance figures dating back three years are essential.
- Qualitative media/journal/trade commentary over the same three-year period would prove useful.
- There is no extra budget allocation and only three people working part-time can be spared for a maximum period of three months.

TABLE 7.2
TYPICAL SOURCES OF DATA

INTERNAL	EXTERNAL
Company library ·	External libraries
Corporate publications	Special reports/surveys
Databases	External databases
Internal surveys	Media broadcasts/reports
Market research	Trade shows/journals
Personal networks	Professional networks
Planning documents	Seminars/conferences
Financial documents	Industry experts/analysts
	Finance houses
	Suppliers/customers
	Company reports
	Business schools/academia
	Consultants
	Trade associations
	Professional institutes

Using these guidelines, it is possible to plan the most appropriate search and collection methods. For example, a lack of any spare budge allocation precludes the possibility of extensive travel or mass surveys to collect information. Appropriate collection methods can be tailored accordingly. Deciding the parameters from the outset lets members of the team know precisely what the constraints are and work proceeds more efficiently.

The task of identifying sources of data is a challenging one. Depending on the selection of potential partners, there will be numerous internal sources or trade associations, industry journals and analysts, surveys and company reports, and so on (see Table 7.2). However, there may be fewer formal channels, including sources such as "what people say." Word of mouth recommendation can be invaluable, whether from friends or media broadcasts. No one person knows all the sources or all the answers. Gathering information is rather like piecing together a jigsaw puzzle; bits in isolation may seem meaningless, but the least significant piece may eventually prove to be the one that completes the picture.

One strength of planning is the freedom it gives people and systems to cope with the unforeseen. A framework for data collection helps not only in collecting the obvious information but enables otherwise seemingly irrelevant details to be put in the picture. Notice how it is that when you have just bought a blue car, there are many other blue cars around? The number does not suddenly increase, merely your awareness of them. Most of the data required already exists; finding it is just a matter of opening eyes and minds and recognizing the essential and the inessential.

The data collection plan should include a list of the internal and/or external data sources to be pursued, by whom, how, and when. Responsibility for collection should be assigned to a named person wherever possible. There are two reasons for this. First, the exercise may continue over an extended period. If a name is attached to each specific element of data collection, there is greater likelihood of the work being handed over when someone is promoted or moved prior to the end of the exercise. Second, it is far easier and more natural for others, whether in the team or not, to communicate or identify with a name than a job title.

The data collection plan should detail the methods by which they are to be collected (for example, by telephone call or survey, personal interview, questionnaire, library visit, etc.). This provides information for others (not necessarily just members of the team) in the short term and a useful reference if the benchmarking exercise is repeated at a later date.

Wherever possible, full details should be included in records of the planning process. This is time consuming and there will inevitably be a temptation to skip some details that "seem obvious" at the time. What is

DON'T DUMP DOCUMENTATION

A bank was faced with major recession in the three areas to which it was most heavily exposed. Profits tumbled. Drastic measures were required to ensure its continued existence.

One initiative introduced as part of a wide-ranging business improvement strategy was "best methods" harmonization. This involved considerable investment over several years and involved key practices in branches across the world. Central to this was detailed analysis of all essential business processes.

The eventual turnaround effected through the improvement strategy became legendary in the industry. Time passed. Staff moved on. Years later, as part of another initiative, processes again came under the microscope. But much of the documentation from the previous exercise had been lost in the intervening period. What could have been a relatively straightforward updating task became instead a major undertaking.

obvious from one perspective can, however, be obscure from another, and clear, comprehensive documentation is always invaluable.

A precise date (day, month and year) by which the information is to be collected should be included in the plan. Vague schedules, such as "mid-July," "end of Quarter 4," are insufficient and open to abuse. When each stage is complete it should be signed off, dated, and other team members advised. This is particularly important because it may affect the work other team members are doing.

When all the planned data have been collected, analysis can begin to determine whether the potential partners originally listed are still relevant, others have been revealed, or no suitable partners can be found.

Worksheet 7 for planning data collection can be found in the Appendix.

8

THE ANALYSIS STAGE

SELECT THE BEST TEAM
ADHERE TO THE ORIGINAL PLAN
BALANCE DATA COLLECTION

A fundamental difference between the planning and analysis stages of benchmarking is that whereas the former is best carried out sequentially—the results of one step determine the course of the next—Steps 5 to 8 are iterative and can be carried out at the same time. This is due not only to the nature of the work involved, but that all teams work in different ways, depending on the mix of skills and strengths represented. What matters in the end is that all the steps are carried out diligently.

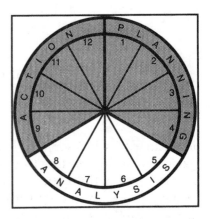

Step 5: Collecting data and selecting partners

In Step 4 the data collection exercise was planned, resources allocated, and responsibilities and methods assigned. This next step is concerned with carrying out this plan, analysing the data, and determining whether they confirm or dismiss the potential partners selected at Step 3.

Whether all, or selected, members of the team are involved in both collection and analysis will depend on the composition of the group. A typical team should include good analytical skills and information search capability—this could involve one or all members (see Table 8.1).

TABLE 8.1
MEMBERS OF THE BENCHMARKING TEAM

A 'typical' benchmarking team is comprised of:

Leader
(who may be the same person as . . .)
Process owner
+
Representation of the following:
Analytical skills
Work process documentation skills
Information search and analysis capability
+
Customer (internal and/or external)
Where and if appropriate

However many of the team are involved, it is important to adhere to the plan, particularly in respect to the completion/review timings. When analyzing information, the temptation is to feel that more data would provide a clearer picture. However, more does not necessarily help, even though yet more could, perceptually, make all the difference. Data collected under such circumstances stand a good change of becoming increasingly spurious or misleading. One reason for fixing time limits to the exercise is to concentrate minds on essentials. Irrelevant and "nice to know" data should be ruthlessly discarded.

Analysis will determine either that it is worthwhile pursuing one or more of the original potential partners; or that none on the original list are of use. In the second case it will be necessary to return to Step 3 and short-list other candidates in the light of what has been discovered. Assuming, however, that there were several potential partners, at least one of these should prove worthy of closer analysis and this, more often than not, will require a visit to the company.

PREPARING A VISIT TO A POTENTIAL BENCHMARK PARTNER

The visit should be the conclusive port of call for information. Unlike competitive analyses, the essence is to comprehend *how* practices result in superior performance. To understand the combination of skills, attitudes, values, pride, and culture that motivate people to produce excellent results, it is necessary to experience them first hand. At least one visit must be made to "get a feel" for how things are done there.

Benchmarking is still relatively new, and it should not be assumed that the partner company will understand the technique, the work involved, or potential benefits. Whether or not a relationship already exists, the initial contact should be carefully thought through. Some useful questions to consider include:

- Do we know this company?
- Who do we know in this company?
- With whom do we need to establish contact (title, level, etc.)?
- How can we clearly explain the purpose of the contact?
- Who is the best person in our organization for this task?

Once this ground has been covered, and before an approach is made, some time should be given to planning a visit in outline. The more care-fully this is thought through, the more convincingly it will communicate and strengthen any resulting association. Questions, shown in Table 8.2, need to be covered at this stage.

When these questions have been addressed, contact can be made and the visit arranged. Depending on the degree of experience or awareness of benchmarking in the proposed partner company, it may be relevant to arrange an initial meeting to explain what is being undertaken and why. Although much of benchmarking is a combination of familiar tools from other performance improvement approaches, the philosophy that under-pins it is countercultural to the behavior of some traditional organizations. During the initial approach, therefore, the cooperative element should be

TABLE 8.2
QUESTIONS TO CONSIDER WHEN PREPARING A VISIT

What	—	is the objective?
Why	—	did your choose this partner?
What	—	is in it for them?
What	—	process do you wish to see?
Where	—	do you wish to visit (office/work site/plant)?
Who	—	is/are the key person/s?
When	—	is it best to visit?
How	—	many people (your team and theirs) will need to be involved?
How	—	long is the envisaged visit (hours/days)?

TABLE 8.3
THE SEARCH FOR INFORMATION

When seeking information:

- Be honest and open about your purpose.
- Do not misrepresent yourself or your company.
- Never ask for something you would not be happy to give in return if asked.
- Offer and be prepared to sign a confidentiality agreement.
- Agree from the outset on any information that may not be requested (particularly if benchmarking with competitors).
- Offer and be prepared to share findings with the partner(s).

TABLE 8.4
ATTITUDES DURING THE VISIT

During the visit:
- The question uppermost in the mind should be how is this done?
- Focus attention on matter of immediate concern. Do not succumb to information "grazing."
- If what is seen or heard is not understood—ask.
- Consciously try to feel behind the visible for the hidden attitudes/skills/values that provide vital clues to superior performance.

stressed, including any mutual benefits that could result, a readiness to share any information gathered, and the lessons to be learned.

There are no formal "visiting" rules, but a general code of conduct has developed based on maintaining an honest, courteous, and respectful manner in benchmark dealings. If there is a guiding principle it is the Golden Rule: "Do unto others as you would have them do unto you" (see Table 8.3).

The groundwork complete, preparations can be made for the visit. Thoroughly completing this beforehand allows a focus on "looking and learning" on site. Preparation should include:

- Understand fully what is being sought and consider the questions that may need to be asked. (It is helpful to write a self-prompt question-naire team members can refer to during the visit.)
- Take the correct people on the visit. This should always include the process owner, but it is wise also to take an informed "observer" who will see and hear objectively.
- Assess hidden values and obtain a feel for what is essential. Be sure to include people with empathy and good listening skills in the visit team.

To make best use of time available during the visit, send the host company details of the areas and topics of interest for analysis and discussion. This allows the host to have the relevant information to hand and field the most suitable people for the meeting.

The purpose of the visit is to gather details of the practices in place and understand how tasks are completed. In rare instances, the difference between your approach to a process and that of the host will be visible immediately. A tour of the plant may reveal a revolutionary piece of loading equipment, for example. More often, however, performance differences depend on a combination of subtle factors (see Table 8.4).

Ask for quantitative data to substantiate what is happening, but avoid the temptation to information "graze." It is easy to be side-tracked or overwhelmed by novelty; adhere rigidly to the plan and you are still likely to come away with more ideas than you bargained for.

By the end of the visit, the team should feel confident of being able to assess the blend of factors that effects superior performance at the host company. For complex processes, more than one visit may be necessary to complete the picture.

On rare occasions, despite evidence of better practices and processes, it may be impracticable to proceed to benchmarking with a company that has been visited. The reason could be that the cultures are too dissimilar: maybe the quality program in one company is too far ahead of the other, or one is part of a multinational group while the other is a small private company. If signs of potential culture clash or language barriers are apparent either in the early stages of the visit or subsequent negotiations, it is preferable to agree not to pursue the matter. Mutually rewarding partnerships rarely develop where values are unevenly matched.

After the visit, the most immediate task is to document the facts and perceptions gathered. The sooner this is done the better because even overnight the initial ideas, perceptions, and feelings will be subtly influenced by the subconscious. Xerox Corporation teams, for example, write their report immediately following the visit, regardless of what time of day that may be. It is far better to use the facilities of a hotel near the benchmark company than wait for everyone to meet in the office the next day.

The task should not be delegated to any single member of the visit team. Each person will have a view that is valuable. Before compiling the final draft of the visit report all members should contribute their views— possibly during a brainstorm-type session—at the group's meeting point. Of particular importance to note are key, or frequently repeated, words that may provide the clues to superior performance.

There are four key areas to cover in the report.

- **Difference in process:** These are the practices involved in performing the actual process.
- **Differences in management:** These are the differences that apply across the range of systems and support practices, such as staffing, skill levels, shift type and number, and resource allocation.
- **Differences in structure:** These include the nature of the organization, whether it is a private or public company, centralized or decentralized, etc. It also includes location (city center or suburban) and age of structural facilities, etc., that will influence the level and type of costs incurred.
- **Differences in culture:** These embody "the way things are done around here." Management may be autocratic, paternalistic, or participative. Doors may be open or firmly closed. First names may predominate or titles be *de riguer.* The atmosphere could be cool, courteous, and professional; warm, vibrant, and entrepreneurial; or cold, studious, and exclusive.

A well-written visit report performs as a vital role during later communications. It complements other desk research data with "live" facts. These provide a human dimension to staff presentations, for example, or anecdotal material for internal publications or wider media use. One good factual report of better performance can win over more skeptics than a host of metrics. Depending on the degree of support for change internally, it may be useful to "float" the report in front of a devil's advocate or band of disbelievers. This will provide the opportunity to see the findings through other people's eyes. Arguments, explanations, and descriptions can be tested before presenting them to one or more of the ultimate decision makers.

STEP 6: DETERMINE THE GAP COMPARED TO THE BENCHMARK

The prime objective during the visit is to complement and/or validate data collected from other courses in order to establish causes of performance difference between your organization and the benchmark company. A visit also ensures that like is being compared with like. Siting and size of plant, number of filling lines, physical structures, and so on will be obvious immediately. While collecting data prior to the visit, assumptions will have been made (an accounting system may define a month as 28 or 30 days, or a calendar month, for example); these could be overturned completely by witnessing another procedure at first hand.

To determine the gap, information must be compiled to provide the basis for analysis and measurement. "What gets measured gets improved." Activities must be measurable before they can stimulate change. The methods chosen for measuring the gap between the existing and the superior performance should reflect the ongoing, long-term nature of benchmarking. The aim should be for clarity and simplicity so that measures will be sustainable and capable of interpretation even by those not involved with the exercise.

It is equally essential to select a practical number of appropriate measures. Figure 8.1 shows those derived by one company following rigorous analysis of its situation. These provided the basis for benchmarking.

"Hard" quantitative differences are relatively straightforward to identify or calculate. Figures can be displayed graphically using standard analysis models, such as pie charts, bar charts, histograms, and so on (see Table 8.5).

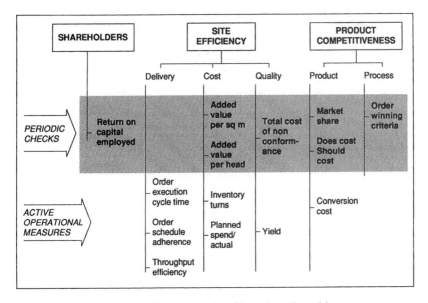

FIGURE 8.1: One example of benchmark architecture

TABLE 8.5:
ANALYZING PERFORMANCE

Methods of analysis:
- Six-word analysis (how, when, why, which, where, who).
- Force field analysis.
- Flow charts.
- Bar charts.
- Histograms.
- Pie charts.
- Scatter diagrams.

Any system or activity conducted by an enterprise can be described by a simple process model, such as the one shown in Figure 8.2. Measurements can be made at certain points:

- The input stage.
- During the work process or activity.
- The output stage.
- On the results.
- On the feedback loop.

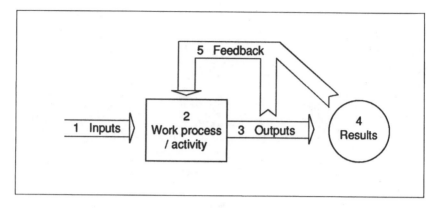

FIGURE 8.2: Process measurement points

Depending on the process in question measurements may be taken from one or more of these points. For example, customer service could be observed at:

Point 1: Stock in warehouse.
Point 3: Accuracy of delivery.
Point 5: The customer's perception of service.

OUTPUT INDICATORS OF QUALITATIVE PERFORMANCE

Good working atmosphere—gaps could be established by measuring:

- Labor turnover over a fixed period.
- Reward and recognition systems (levels/frequency/reviews).
- Off-site or on-the-job training per person per year (days/spend).
- Number/variety of shared social events.
- Employee well-being initiatives (canteen/healthcare etc.).

Satisfied customers—gaps could be established by measuring:

- Number/type of complaints.
- Number of repeat orders.
- Technical backup (team/specific initiatives).
- Average "age" of customer relationships.
- Special promotion packages (number/type).

Good benchmarking combines a measurement of quantitative and qualitative data. A means of deriving numeric comparisons from visual or perceptual information is, therefore, required to determine what else accounts for performance gaps. For each intangible comparison, such as "better working atmosphere" or "more satisfied customers" indicators can be found from which numeric outputs are derived.

Where these are not immediately obvious, a numeric interpretation may be found by returning to the previous step. Most of the intangible information will flow from points 4 (Results) and 5 (Feedback), and suitable measures will often be found at 3 (Outputs). In some cases, however, it may be necessary to go back as far as 1 (Inputs) to find a "measurable" factor.

No matter how obscure the qualitative information, measurables can always be found by this backtracking mechanism. Some of the indicators will be more apt or useful than others. Initially, it is best to list as many as possible and gradually draw out and emphasize the few that are most meaningful (see Figure 8.3).

Once suitable measures have been established, the gap analysis can be produced. This should be an objective assessment of the size and nature of the performance difference. Gaps are referred to as POSITIVE when the *internal* practices produce a *better* performance than comparative ones; or NEGATIVE when the *internal* practices produce a *worse* performance than comparative ones.

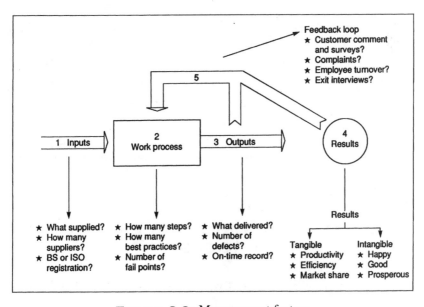

FIGURE 8.3: Measurement factors

In the early stages, most gaps will be negative. However, when benchmarking is the norm or reaches a stage of maturity within the organization, some may be positive. This is quite feasible. It is possible that a component of a process, internally considered capable of improvement, is nonetheless better than that of the partner. This will not necessarily be apparent until the analysis is carried out. Experience indicates that this quite commonly occurs and leads to positive benefit for the partner, who will be able to improve that part of the process. Sometimes a joint decision is taken to seek a "best practice" third party comparison for this element. This then forms the basis of a separate exercise (and incidentally accounts for development of benchmarking networks).

Also, as programs roll through the organization, there will be performance improvements in areas not formally benchmarked. These will be recognized only when attention is focused on them.

Whether the bias is negative or positive, the gap analysis should include:

- Tables providing descriptive and numeric data on both benchmark and existing processes.
- A calculation of the size of the gap.
- An explanation of the most feasible possible causes.
- An assessment of the scope/nature of changes that would be required to close the gap and exceed the benchmark performance.
- Priority of these to produce optimum improvement.
- Evaluation of suitability/practicability of implementation.
- Time-frame and cost assessment.
- Conclusions and recommendations.
- A graphic illustration of the performance gap (see Figure 8.4).

The gap analysis is fundamental to the later communications plan (see Step 9) and should avoid use of jargon or hyperbole. The graphic display should be clear, uncluttered, and capable of interpretation across all levels of the organization.

STEP 7: ESTABLISH DIFFERENCES IN PROCESS

The experience of mapping out your process will be invaluable during this step.

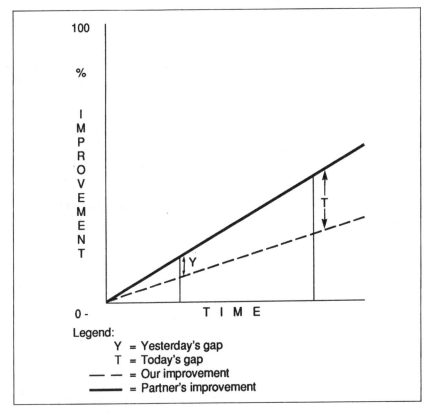

FIGURE 8.4: Displaying the performance gap

The clearest and most comprehensive way to highlight differences is by direct visual comparison. It would be an extraordinary stroke of luck to find that a map of the benchmark process already exists at the partner company. It is more likely that your team will have to draw it. For complex processes, numerous discussions may be necessary before it is complete. However, it is essential to have as comprehensive a picture as possible, and there is nothing to be gained from short-circuiting this procedure (see Figure 8.5).

When complete, the map can be displayed side by side with that of the existing process, preferably close to where the process takes place. The differences should be clearly highlighted. A third map can then be drawn depicting clearly the alterations or adjustments and how the process will look following integration of these. Where only minor alterations are to be

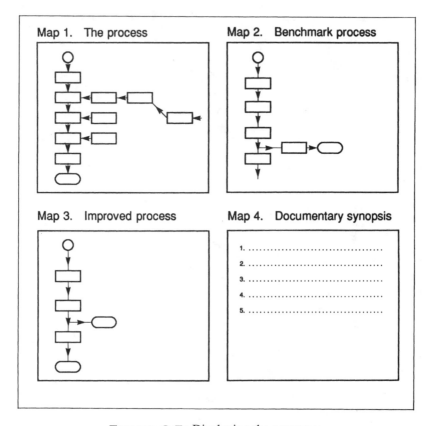

FIGURE 8.5: Displaying the processes

made, it is easier to draw enlarged versions of those sections to be affected rather than the whole.

The maps should be accompanied by a documentary synopsis of the changes together with the dates when they are to be implemented and completed.

While the maps will show the actual process differences and laterations, the most difficult elements to differentiate will be those associated with the intangible factors. Attitude, paradigm, and culture differences cannot be shown on the map nor can they be adopted wholesale. For this reason, documenting what was seen and felt promptly following the visit is vital. There may be key concepts or factors that could be incorporated in other ongoing quality or training initiatives to secure longer-term improvement. An indication of these, or any other knock-on effects of the benchmarking visit, should be included in the synopsis.

Step 8: Target future performance

Having graphically displayed the gap in performance (Step 6), this now needs to be extrapolated forward to plan future performance. However, traditional target setting is inappropriate and insufficient in today's dynamic environment. Whatever difference now exists between the best practice and any other will expand through momentum even if the best practice company does nothing extra. Because best practice rarely occurs without conscious effort, it is probable that companies achieving it will continue to improve at an ever-increasing rate rather than standing still.

Displaying the future position, both conservatively and potentially, will help in setting targets that take the company to a position of superiority in its industry. It is impossible to know precisely what will happen in time, but a scenario based on the impact of reasonable assumptions can be illustrated (see Figure 8.6).

WHEN CALCULATING THE GAP

- Never make assumptions about the future based purely on the past or present—allow for what may happen tomorrow.
- To make up for the present gap, the rate of improvement over the target period must be greater than the benchmark partner's.
- The benchmark partner's rate of improvement also will increase even if it does nothing extra.

This suggests that targets set for your company's future performance must be well beyond the current gap. The reaction they provoke should be one of incredulity rather than speculation.

Key points to bear in mind are:

- The gap exists because performance varies.
- Only past and present performance can be known.
- Extrapolating historic performance forward inevitably expands the gap at the same rate.

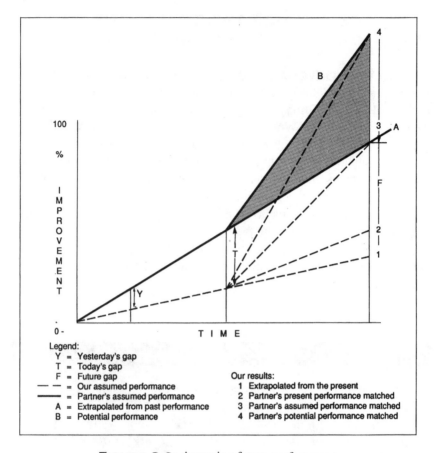

FIGURE 8.6: Assessing future performance

- The poorer performer, being behind from the outset, must increase the rate of improvement by a greater amount than the better performer just to maintain the gap.
- The better performer is likely to improve at an increasing rate.
- The poorer performer must make a significant improvement leap in order to close the gap.
- To leap ahead, the poorer performer must improve by an amount representing the initial lag, plus the performance difference today, plus an estimate of the future potential gap, plus an extra contingency figure to allow for major breakthroughs at the benchmark company over the projected period.

"We already have enough ideas in place to double our rate of improvement over the next five years" Chairman: Toyota

It is essential, therefore, to set targets beyond those achieved by the benchmark company, because it will not stand still. Even in the time it takes to complete the analysis, your partner already may have moved ahead.

9

THE ACTION STAGE

COMMUNICATION IS ESSENTIAL

FOLLOW THROUGH DETERMINES SUCCESS

MONITOR PROGRESS AND UPDATE

It is in this stage that information and knowledge gathered during planning and analysis is converted into efforts that will result in improved performance. This is not guaranteed. A manual can, at best, describe only what should be done if achievement is to have a chance. It is the diligent follow-through that determines success, or failure of the program.

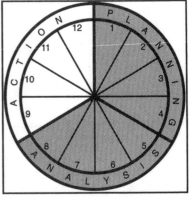

Planning and analysis are largely passive activities involving relatively few people; it is possible to halt the exercise temporarily or permanently at any stage with little deleterious effect. Conversely, the further the program rolls into the action stage, the more difficult it is to stop. It is similar to pressing the emergency switch on a moving train; the train speeds up as it moves out of the station and the greater the distance traveled the more serious the effects will be.

Without exception, all managers proactive in benchmarking stress the importance of total commitment. This must be demonstrated by all those involved in the exercise. However, it is at the action stage that senior management commitment is particularly crucial if large-scale resources or changes are required.

This, therefore, is the vital ingredient for success during Stage 3. All action plans should be formulated in the context of gaining and sustaining wholehearted commitment.

The action steps, as in Stage 2, are iterative. Moreover, because many of them will have a resultant, often ongoing ripple effect through the organization, it is essential to ensure regular monitoring and updating mechanisms are built in from the outset.

The more positive and efficient the execution of introductory action steps, the greater will be the potential for improvement over the longer term.

STEP 9: COMMUNICATE BENCHMARK FINDINGS

As Chapter 3 indicates, benchmarking can be instrumental in promoting the climate for change. It is, however, only one of a series of initiatives that can be employed to affect broad reform. With any TQM or change program, whether or not consequent action plans are adopted, smooth progress depends on communication. Carefully planned and sensitively executed, it can secure commitment and gain cooperation.

People can be naturally resistant or reluctant to adopt new practices, and this must be overcome before implementation. The first stage of the communication program, prior to introducing any new initiatives, should cascade the background and findings of the benchmarking exercise through the organization to gain this commitment. Belief in the need for change and the willingness to undertake it will be much enhanced if people receive a clear, positive message.

It is probable in the early stages that only those directly involved with the exercise will know or understand what has been happening. Communications should therefore provide detailed reasons for benchmarking as well as opportunities, plans, and objectives for the future. Where practicable, visual aids, such as posters, or overheads, should be used to support and highlight key points. Many companies have bulletin boards (mostly ignored when they contain only pages on procedures and policies) that are ideal for punchy bulleted messages. Audio tapes provide an effective medium for people whose work involves "spare" learning time in cars (sales and technical service staff, for example).

The consequences of benchmarking will be most keenly felt by those whose jobs are directly affected. In addition to a carefully constructed general communications program, particular attention should be focused on these individuals or groups.

When designing the communications program, it is important to consider:

• Who is most affected by what has been discovered?
• How will this affect them?

Everyone reacts differently to the prospect of change; some people welcome the challenge, others feel uncomfortable or apprehensive about its effects, while a minority strongly resist it. Communications must be sympathetic and appeal to the whole range of feeling. Strong resistance sometimes can be overcome by involving the person or people in a visit to the benchmark company. On witnessing better practice, the resentment associated with being told something better can be achieved is often dissolved. This is particularly so if the result of improving the work is seen to be making it cleaner, simpler, or more enjoyable; as well as more efficient.

Cooperation is the second requirement in bringing about change; extraordinary amounts may be essential to achieve superior performance. In addition to securing commitment, therefore, the communications program should prepare the basis for teamwork and collaboration. The exact nature of this will depend on the culture and style of the organization. An effec-

BUZZ GROUPS!

When people, systems, and companies are working well and achieving excellent results, they exude a positive, often contagious, energy. The "buzz" may vary from stimulating to inspirational. One company, before involving any new people in its benchmarking program, regularly sends them on a tour of the partner company's premises. The objective is to "feel and see" at first hand the atmosphere and conditions that exist when work is being done to the best of people's ability. Described as "rolling the last few feet of a suspense film first," they maintain that this provides the extra impetus and inspiration needed to cope with any difficulty, disruption, or drama along the journey to improvement.

tive program will, however, include consideration of key factors listed below.

Communications should include:

• A vision of the future.
• What benchmarking is and how it fits in with this.
• The benefits to be gained.
• Why benchmarking is being implemented.
• Which process is being examined and why.
• The name of the process owner(s).
• How and why the benchmark partners were selected.
• The quantitative and qualitative benchmarks.

Communications should also address the following issues:

• What are the benefits to the individual?
• What is the goal?
• What is the time frame?
• Who will be involved?
• Why and when will they be involved?
• How will they be involved?

All too often, new initiatives run out of steam after the initial flurry of activity. Life settles back to normal and inertia creeps in. Renewed injections of enthusiasm and support are required to prevent this. Progress must be reported regularly and on a recurring basis—not just when spectacular strides are made—so that everyone can share in the achievement. Such reports should encompass:

• Which milestones have been reached.
• What has been accomplished so far (factual and anecdotal).
• What the next milestones are.
• Review of targets (especially if these have been altered in any way).

Once the concept and practice of benchmarking have been accepted internally, the communications program should broaden to include external "listeners." While some managers may be reluctant, good benchmarking companies talk openly and keenly about their experience and progress. AT&T goes further by offering its benchmarking workshops to the general public.

Seminars and conferences provide excellent opportunities for dissemination of experiences as well as for encouraging potential benchmark partners. A senior executive with Digital Equipment Corporation regularly gives benchmarking presentations at international conferences and invites members of the audience to drop their business cards in a box if they wish to know more about the subject generally or networks in particular.

Similar initiatives may broaden the external perception of managers while multiplying the number of channels for new ideas to flow into the organization.

STEP 10: ADJUST GOALS AND DEVELOP CORRECTIVE IMPROVEMENT PLAN

Incremental improvement can be achieved using the old remedies. Quantum leaps forward require the strength of purpose to go for bold goals, which are rarely attained without discomfort or even an amount of pain. Sometime this is coupled with an extraordinary leap of faith.

THE LIGHT FANTASTIC

Nissan Motor set a bold goal for its bulb suppliers: a maximum of one defect in 10 million within seven years. At the time the industry average defect rate was 1 per 100.

However, Nissan did not disclose its ultimate goal from the outset. Selecting its best bulb supplier (Philips), it set the target of one defect per 1,000. When this was achieved, it moved the goalposts to one per 10,000; then one per 100,000; then one per million. Each time Nissan moved the goalposts, no matter how impossible it seemed, Philips was determined to reach it until the final one in 10 million was achieved.

Everyone was delighted, especially Philips. When Nissan disclosed that this had been its goal from the outset, Philips' managers asked how the Japanese company had known it could be possible. "You were our best supplier of bulbs, so we knew that if anyone could do it you could, even though we didn't know how you were going to get there," was the reply.

It is this order of faith that accompanies bold goals.

As in this example, once the strategy is formulated, a plan to achieve it must be developed. It is easy to underestimate our, and other people's, potential; drawing out the best is usually only possible through a combination of vision—to recognize potential and patience—to nurture its development. First teach people to climb, then ask them to scale Pike's Peak!

The more ambitious the goal, the more flexible that initial target must be. The unique feature of benchmarking is the comparison with actual "best practice" performance. This gives a realistic reflection of what is ultimately, if not immediately, achievable.

Adjusting the goals requires setting milestones commensurate with people's ability; at the same time providing realistic yardsticks that stretch but do not break them. Individuals need and respond to challenges. However, they buckle or rebel if asked to undertake the impossible without the requisite tools, or the freedom to enable ingenuity to find a way. The more effort that is demanded, or responsibility devolved, the greater the support, training, and guidance needed.

The achievement of goals does not depend solely on the willingness or skill of individuals. Goals must be sufficiently flexible to allow for continual minor adjustment in the light of new information. This may result from extrinsic factors such as fluctuations in the political climate or feedback from customers, or intrinsically from leadership changes, inconsistencies in performance, or changing budgetary considerations. Goals should constantly be synchronized to such feedback to ensure they remain realistic.

Excellent contingency planning and information management are the hallmarks of best practice; equally, they are undoubtedly major components in attaining landmark goals.

At the same time, it is important to implement a corrective improvement plan. This is:

- A solution or change suggested by data collection and analysis;
- A plan to implement the change or solution; and
- A method to monitor/check/review impact on outputs, results, and critical success factors.

The corrective improvement plan is the set of actions to effect the solution. It incorporates the means to review and monitor progress toward the goal, and the impact of benchmarking activities on critical success factors.

It is crucial to identify and secure the commitment of those whose support is essential in the early stages of implementation. Additionally, this momentum must be maintained over the longer term. There is a difference between:

- Active commitment, which is required from those involved in carrying out the improvements; and
- Passive commitment from those who must be relied on to provide essential background support (such as sanctioning expenditure).

Successful implementation will stand or fall according to the degree of engagement of all these people.

Essential check questions to ask before formulating the improvement plan are:

- Is the collated information comprehensive and accurate?
- Can it be trusted?
- Are the benchmarked processes measurably better?
- Are the changes necessary to improve existing practices commensurate with the available ability?
- Do the changes accord with existing values?

The answers must always be positive. Assuming this is so, the task must be to generate the optimum plan and implementation procedures. Where necessary (for example where capital expenditure is needed), these should include securing relevant approvals.

There are no golden rules for procedure. The way things are done will be influenced by prevailing attitudes and culture. However, the following suggests some general guidelines.

CORRECTIVE IMPROVEMENT PLAN: GENERAL GUIDELINES

- Decide on the criteria to judge solutions.
- Balance long-term solutions with short-term gain.
- Generate as many solutions as possible and as many potential reasons why they might fail.
- Select the most appropriate solution.
- Agree on master implementation and monitoring plan.
- Split into manageable steps with built-in contingency.
- Identify whose (active and passive) commitment is required.
- Communicate clearly to everyone involved.
- Agree and draw up individual action plans for those directly involved in implementation—these should incorporate unambiguous goals and deadlines.

- Set up an uncomplicated monitoring and reporting system.
- Ensure everyone clearly understands the process, evaluation criteria, and communication lines applicable when these are achieved.

Worksheet 8 showing a sample action plan can be found in the Appendix.

STEP 11: IMPLEMENT CORRECTIVE IMPROVEMENT PLAN

No amount of reading, writing, or exhortation will secure successful implementation. There are no quick fixes or easy answers, no magic wands or secret solutions. There is only the guarantee that the accolade of "best" will not be achieved through one solitary action. Two factors, however, that can help determine success are: detailed attention and attention to detail.

When all the hype is stripped away from the debate about what made Japanese firms pre-eminent, their obsession with detail is the one common denominator that stands out. Assuming that communications strategies have established secure foundations, attention to detail will be the one factor that governs the outcome of any implementation plan. A question that frequently occupies the minds of would-be benchmarkers is how an already excellent company can stay ahead if everyone else is benchmarking against it, the implication being that their methods then become just average. The truth is that while many seek and find best practice, few companies are sufficiently adept in detailed, attentive follow-through to overtake the leaders. Furthermore, outstanding performers are rarely complacent. They continue to hone their competitive edge and so increase their potential for staying in front.

During implementation, attention should focus on:

- The process being improved.
- Progress of the improvement plan.

In Step 7 (Establish differences in process), maps were drawn showing the differences between the existing and the best practice processes and highlighting the changes required. During implementation the desired changes should be effected in the agreed sequence and carefully monitored. Major changes should be implemented on a reduced (test) basis for a period and only scaled up when success is proved. For example, when initiating major accounting system changes, these could be tested at one location before being implemented across the company. The general procedure is as follows. (See also Figure 9.1).

- Try out the new process for the planned (or test) period.
- Monitor and measure results to determine whether the change is working.
- Document all changes.
- Communicate initial results.
- Plan further improvement.
- Implement and monitor.
- Document.
- Communicate.

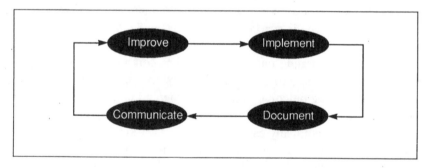

FIGURE 9.1: The route for successful improvement

When all the planned changes are in place, redraw the final process map and display it in a suitably prominent place.

Monitoring progress during the improvement plan must allow for the unforeseen as well as the planned agenda. This means:

- Maintaining the commitment of everyone affected by or involved in implementation. Most programs will take at least weeks, if not months, to implement, and over this time enthusiasm is bound to wane if not constantly fueled by success stories (no matter how small), praise, and other signs of recognition and appreciation.
- Frequent and enthusiastic communication of progress and achievements throughout the organization.
- Review of contingency plans and deadlines.

- Modifying the plan as suggested by unforeseen or unexpected developments.
- Constant monitoring and review of progress.
- Concise and precise documentation of improvements.

When the benchmark goal has been achieved . . .
Tell the world!

then . . .

Set bolder goals!

STEP 12: REVIEW PROGRESS AND CALIBRATE

Review is to benchmarking as breathing is to life. It is so obviously necessary that it is often taken for granted. Many people only breathe efficiently and effectively when they are made aware of bad habits; shallow breathing, for example, can compound the effects of tiredness or stress, whereas deep breathing helps combat them.

Similarly with review. It is essential, but how many people have a disciplined procedure? The necessity for this, in the context of the overall benchmarking process, is discussed in detail in the following chapter. However, because it is also the concluding step in each exercise, it is covered briefly here.

During the 12-step process, there are several points at which it is advisable to take an objective look at progress. In Step 5, for instance, where, if no partner is found, several or all of the previous steps must be recycled.

The final review at Step 12 has a different quality. The main question to be raised is: "Have we met our objectives for this benchmarking exercise?"

If the review procedure has been thorough during successive stages, then the answer to this should be positive. However, this should not be assumed. A final review session must be conducted. Preferably, a provisional date for this will be fixed well in advance to alert essential attendees to reserve the time. The meeting should include representatives from the team, the work process and executive management. Apart from analyzing whether the original objective has been met, attention needs to focus on performance improvement of the benchmark partner's process. Depending on the length of time taken for the benchmarking exercise, other potential partners will possibly have improved also. As seen in Step 8, the world does not stop revolving while one person benchmarks.

Some guidelines for the Step 12 review are suggested below.

- Fix a provisional review date at the outset when objectives are agreed and commitment is high.
- Confirm this as soon as is reasonable; if left too near the end of the exercise, the danger is that people will be too busy fighting the next battle.
- In addition to your process, ensure that evidence is available of external practices other than just the benchmark.
- Consider the following questions:

  — Have the objectives been met?
  — What is the evidence of improvement?
  — How high is commitment?
  — If high, is it sustainable?
  — Was the exercise efficient and effective?

- What needs to be done to improve benchmarking skills before the next benchmarking exercise?
- Is there a need for (more) training?
- Is our process now where we want it to be?
- Can it be placed on the back burner and attention turned elsewhere?
- Or is further work required?
- Who is the ongoing process champion?
- What mechanism is in place to maintain the improvement/signal the need for further improvement in the future?
- How effective have communications been?
- Have benchmarking approaches in respect to this process been received from other organizations?
- How can we become still more outward looking?
- When should this process be reviewed again?

The review session should supply evidence and information on which to base decisions about future courses of action. There may be instances during the introductory phase of benchmarking when it is necessary to recycle the whole exercise because objectives have not been met. This usually will become more apparent during, rather than at the end of, the 12-step process.

When benchmarking is integrated into the culture, the final review will provide evidence of the results of desired improvement on business performance. The key factor then is to build regular formal review in the ongoing management procedures to avoid possible regression. Depending on the level of the process, a suitable opportunity might be afforded during annual performance assessment/objective setting with the process owner or at the senior executive business strategy planning session.

10

MAINTAINING LEADERSHIP

INTERNAL AUDIT MARKS PROGRESS

NEW INFORMATION ADDS DYNAMISM

EXECUTIVE IN CHARGE OF BUSINESS REVIEWS

The need for change and improvement, if not welcomed, is at least justifiable when the competitive climate is grim and the economic cycle is at its lowest point. However, those companies riding the crest of a wave with booming profits could be forgiven for putting change near the bottom of the list of priorities. "We're doing OK as we are, so don't rock the boat!" is a familiar phrase. But complacency can lead to downfall, as the Swiss discovered.

For example, geography has played a major role in Switzerland's industrial development. The high proportion of land unsuitable for cultivation has, over the centuries, led to an economy more reliant on trade and industry than agriculture. Moreover, widely dispersed settlements encouraged livelihoods dependent on crafts and skills handed down through generations. Legendary among these was, of course, watch and clock making. In the towns around Geneva, this industry had, by the nineteenth century, given the Swiss a global monopoly. Swiss watches were synonymous with excellence until well into the mid-twentieth century. By the second half of this century, however, a member of the Swiss watchmaking fraternity was experimenting with non-traditional "movements." Eventually he devised a working model with no jewels or mainspring and yet was an accurate timepiece. With pride he presented his revolutionary new technology at the annual Horologists Convention where he expected it to meet with enthusiasm and wonder.

Instead, the reaction was shock and incomprehension. How could *anyone,* and a Swiss at that, call something with no jewels, levers, or complex movements, a watch? The idea was dismissed with perfunctory civility. By the Swiss. Yet several years later, Seiko took the world by storm and almost overnight demolished the Swiss monopoly. Today it is impossible to image a world without the quartz watch.

Success, as this example shows, breeds within it the seeds of its own destruction. Time and again, a single good idea revolutionizes years of tradition and practice. Of course, if that idea is your country's or company's, then you are laughing. If not . . .

In the late 1980s, Tom Peters and Bob Waterman published their landmark book that probably did more to spark the current quality/customer debate than any other. Since then, *In Search of Excellence* has become almost better known as a record of "Those were the great that were," which conveys no disrespect of the companies that have subsequently run into doldrums. Their fate could be anybody's.

Having climbed the ladder to excellence, or, as in the case with benchmarking, the 12 Steps to be World Best, how can companies avoid the seemingly inevitable slippery slide into the abyss on the other side? Excellent management of the business and its resources is obviously essential; a number of estimable tests recently published give clues to achieving this. Additional impetus is provided by the continuous review and improvement ethos that is built into benchmarking.

As an increasing number of processes come under the benchmarking microscope, more and more people are trained in the philosophy of review as an integral part of continuous improvement. Hence, over time it becomes second nature to a growing percentage of the organization's population. Unfortunately, relying on this notion alone to maintain best performance in what inevitably will be a progressively fierce competitive arena is insufficient.

RECALIBRATING THE COMPANY

Formal reviews of processes that have attained benchmark status should be carried out at annual intervals, most logically as part of the business planning cycle. Often referred to as "recalibration," this centers on: reviewing the measurements of benchmarked processes to ensure they are still valid in the light of any external changes, and reassessing the penetration of the benchmarking philosophy throughout the organization.

As with all benchmarking activities, the most effective method is to start with an internal audit. This is followed by revising the best practice partner to establish how far it has progressed. (Gathering information from other than the partner company is part of a broader, ongoing "excellence" review.)

The internal audit should gauge the extent to which gaps exist in the benchmark information, their nature and scope (these could be new gaps that have been revealed during the exercise, or original information gaps never satisfactorily closed—possibly due to cultural or other exigencies or because they were not considered critical); and whether, and by how much, attitudes toward and understanding of benchmarking have changed since the exercise was completed or last reviewed.

Having detailed and up-to-date knowledge in these internal areas gives greater purpose to the external aspects of the review. It will be necessary in most cases to carry out some kind of employee attitude survey to ascertain this knowledge. This may vary in scope from all-embracing, formal questionnaires to informal face-to-face sample interviews, or inclusion as a small part of another survey. Much will depend on the culture of the organization, and the "age" of the benchmarking program.

Seeking new or challenging information adds a dynamic dimension to checking previously gathered and recorded data. The experience and benefit of hindsight play a vital role in the recalibration process. Even if the data and information are the same, they may be subject to different interpretations after, as opposed to before, the integration of benchmarking.

Additionally, feedback from the attitude survey will help keep the direction and focus of the company's benchmarking approach in tune with the perceptions and development of its people and with their acceptance and understanding of the new philosophy. It will highlight areas of weakness or misdirection, indicating where greater emphasis is needed. This in turn helps in the allocation of resources to those areas where the most impact will be felt.

So far, two aspects of review have been covered:

• As the twelfth step in each benchmarking exercise.
• As an ongoing iterative component of the process and progress of benchmarking within the company.

INTERNAL AUDIT: THE ACCEPTANCE OF BENCHMARKING

When undertaking an internal audit, the following points should be considered:

- How important is benchmarking in strategy planning?
- How far is this reflected in annual business planning?
- How far is it incorporated into individual objectives?
- Of what value is benchmarking perceived to have added to business and resource management?
- Is the systematic process understood?
- How much training is being given in the technique?
- How much refresher training is being given on a needs basis?
- In which areas are learning most required?
- How are acceptance, understanding, and value of benchmarking measured? How much have they increased since the previous review?
- What improvements are being made to the benchmarking process?

To complete the review in terms of maintaining leadership, a third aspect must be considered:

- The panoramic overview or reconnaissance of worldwide best practices.

This is quite distinct from the everyday running of the business. This responsibility should be held by someone well equipped to identify, interpret, and translate best practices in the context of their impact on the mission and vision of the company. Such an individual will probably, but not necessarily, be a member of the senior executive team.

THE BUSINESS REVIEW EXECUTIVE

This can be assisted by the appointment of a business review executive (BRE). This person has expert knowledge of the company's processes and systems; access to a well-constructed global network of leading-edge thinkers in academia, marketing, science, and technology; and a restless creative mind with boundless energy and enthusiasm for positive change and continuous improvement. Contrary to the boisterous image this may conjure up, the suitable personality is as likely to be a self-reliant quiet thinker and listener with detailed understanding of the corporate architecture.

The person selected for this role would be expected to:

- Have expert knowledge of company processes and systems.
- Have a thorough grasp of the corporate architecture.
- Have access to a global network of leading-edge thinkers in business and academia.
- Have positive energy and enthusiasm for change.
- Constantly question the status quo, challenging perceptions and exploding paradigms.
- Have an inquiring mind, coupled with energy and enthusiasm.
- Be proactive and externally focused.
- Be a creative, lateral, but practical thinker.
- Become the corporation bee, constantly cross-fertilizing internal ideas and best practices with those seen and heard outside the organization.

And finally, because the change agent is not acclimated to the impact of change:

- The individual should fulfill this role for a maximum of three years.

Up to three-quarters of the BREs work output—to be the global eyes and ears of the company—is conducted away from the office. Through a distillation of leading-edge thinking, writing, and practice, the executive is responsible for feeding back into the organization that which may enhance its performance.

The balance of the output is conducted back at the base. Liaising at all levels, roaming, questioning, examining, and probing into activities and processes, the role of the BRE is designed to constantly challenge perceptions and explode the organization's paradigms—a supreme devil's advocate. The purpose is to nip complacency in the bud before it has the chance to mature and become dangerous.

Some companies already have such an *agent provocateur* in place. The role encompasses the additional traits needed to keep the organization on its toes and provide it with the highest probability of "seeing" from where opportunities and threats are likely to come.

11

CASE HISTORIES OF BENCHMARKING IN PRACTICE

There is much to be learned from other firms' experiences. This chapter presents seven companies that have introduced benchmarking and have adopted it as one of their strategic management tools.

The cases are drawn from the manufacturing industry, the service sector, and "Third Wave" information technology companies. They include elements of internal, external, and best practice benchmarking. They are not intended as Harvard-type studies but rather as role models. They describe some of the lessons learned, hurdles overcome, and progress achieved.

1. SHELL CHEMICALS UK LTD*

Previous chapters have shown how benchmarking efforts are aided considerably when there is supportive leadership of, and commitment to, continuous improvement from the top of the organization. If focus on the external environment, openness to new ideas, and a willingness to incorporate benchmarking into corporate strategy are added, then the commitment of business and line management will more readily follow.

This has been the experience at Shell Chemicals UK Ltd. (SCUK), one of the major divisions within Shell Transport & Trading, the UK's third-largest company by market capitalization. It is also part of the Royal Dutch/Shell Group which employs 135,000 people worldwide.

In the latter part of 1990, the senior management team at SCUK was assessing a number of techniques that could enhance the company's TQM program. Following considerable research and discussion, it was agreed that benchmarking could provide the rational structure that would help businesses gain optimum improvement and, hence, returns. The responsibility for benchmarking was devolved to the business managers at the end of that year, and during 1991 some 14 benchmarking teams were brought together to analyze and define the company's critical success factors that, in turn, would identify the key processes to which benchmarking could be applied.

Valuable learning points arose even in the early stages. There was undoubted commitment to the technique, and the teams met frequently to identify the areas of value to examine. Despite the considerable energy and effort invested, however, the first few months proved difficult and little visible progress was made.

Analysis of the underlying problem suggested there was insufficient understanding of *how* to benchmark. Original critical success factors proved too large and unfocused and their definition nebulous; consequently, they were difficult to measure. The solution was to develop suitable training for the benchmarking teams.

Rather than reinvent the wheel, SCUK looked for and identified organizations that had successfully implemented benchmarking programs. Discussing their experiences and "picking brains" led to a prototype design that was then molded to suit the company's needs and culture. By the middle of the year, workshops were in place to provide the skills the teams required to manage the process.

Throughout 1991 the teams worked to identify, define, and analyze their critical business success factors in light of what had been learned from their

---

*Reprinted from first edition.

workshops. They describe progress during this period as analogous to walking through quicksand—a slow, constant struggle to get anywhere. During this "struggle," however, they learned what others before, and since, also have realized. While the areas selected for benchmarking were deemed to be most useful, they had not necessarily been accurately, or correctly, defined. The challenge was to find the key to each process, acknowledging that the first example found was not always the right one. In other words, they had to keep asking: "Hey! What do we actually mean by that?" This is *the* recurring phrase throughout benchmarking. A business process is like an onion; each layer peeled off reveals yet another layer, and another, and so on.

The constant necessity to analyze, define, and reanalyze operational processes has proved education in itself and of great value to the company. Within a year of setting up the benchmarking program, the teams have reintroduced basic flow chart methodology to break processes down to their *smallest* part to allow the critical factors to be defined and measured accurately. The original "sequential step" model, which provided the foundation for the training, also has evolved into a more fluid version. It now allows for the fact that, in practice, the "steps" may be completed contemporaneously or out of sequence. This does not affect the thoroughness with which each step is completed but may result in shorter cycle times for the benchmarking process.

Other lessons learned are reflected in the following specific example of benchmarking in the business.

One critical area identified at the outset of 1991 was continuity of supply. More specifically, moving some 700,000 tonnes of feedstocks to chemical plants throughout the UK. Limited logistics and storage necessitate detailed planning of this operation. Discontinuity of supply can result in plants having to shut down; this is costly and fraught with problems.

The objective of the benchmarking study was to improve contingency planning. The management team brought together a cross-functional group of eight, drawn from marketing, distribution, finance, and pipeline operations. The first team meeting was followed up with regular sessions to brainstorm critical success factors, conduct flowchart analyses, and identify data required and potential benchmark partners. This work resulted in two companies being selected as suitable contacts.

Planning process data were gathered internally and followed through by contacting the selected companies. Letters sent to key people were followed up over the telephone. The external contacts were keen, in principle, to arrange meetings to discuss the potential gains but were insufficiently aware of the benchmarking technique, or not far enough down the TQM route to understand how it could benefit both parties. SCUK quickly realized that, in addition to developing acceptance of the new philosophy and concept internally, they had to develop similar acceptance in their benchmark companies before work could begin. After many weeks of "education," discussion, and negotiation, however, agreement was reached with the two organizations to share information.

One of these has proved to be very fruitful. Performance gaps, linked to quantitative measurements, have been identified by detailed analysis and process comparison. Where it is of interest to the benchmark partner, the information is freely shared. The cooperative dialogue is keen because the "partner" subsequently identified one of its key processes at which it recognizes SCUK to be "best." This has therefore become the subject of a second benchmarking exercise between the two companies.

Both sides of this partnership have discovered the similarities in culture and management style that have assisted their efforts. This is an unexpected bonus. Superior performance can owe as much to management behavior and attitude as to measurably better processes. No matter how willing companies are to benchmark against each other, efforts can be frustrated, or even abandoned, if the culture and operational climate are found to be too dissimilar.

It is too early to know what operational change may result from the detailed work involved. Sufficient progress has been made, however, to convince SCUK that it will continue down this route and that benchmarking will be one of the quality tools with which it will work to improve performance in key operations. Difficulties encountered, such as those resulting from unfocused targets or defining too wide an output to measure successfully, and the lessons learned are regularly communicated to other businesses through seminars. This is resulting in a clearer understanding of the business and operational processes, as well as of the technique itself, spreading through the organization.

Senior managers at SCUK UK Ltd. recognize that no one person or organization can have a monopoly on all the good ideas. There is much to be learned from establishing good relationships in non-competitive areas. Viewed in this light, they see no limitations to gradually adopting benchmarking in most corporate activities and have no hesitation in recommending its use to others.

While acknowledging that returns will not be apparent overnight, the benchmarking teams now feel that, instead of struggling through quicksand, their path is leading along a fairly firm beach with only occasional flurries of sand blowing in their eyes.

2. DIGITAL EQUIPMENT CORPORATION (DEC)

During the late 1980s the computer industry, like many others, was facing an increasingly harsh environment. The industry itself also was changing as growth slowed and margins shrank. In 1989, Digital Equipment Corporation (DEC) carried out a strategic review at the company's headquarters. This concluded that financial efficiency would become increasingly critical to the success of the business. The corollary to this was to focus on overheads and find areas where significant savings could be made.

A team was chartered to look at work and organization redesign. Its goal was to study the corporation from the outside in, to discover areas where DEC was perceived by outsiders to be best in its class and other areas that offered opportunities for improvement.

The team identified companies and work categories, devised questions, and visited recognized best-in-class companies such as IBM, Canon, Motorola, Sony, Ricoh, and Ford. The justification for looking at a preponderance of Japanese companies was "that was where the toughest competition emanated from." In each case, the team studied financial processes from the organizational (work) and cultural perspectives. Comparing these with their own processes highlighted potential sources of savings in areas including information systems and access, organization, and role structure as well as the financial processes themselves.

Analyzing the findings led to a choice of three possible scenarios:

- Significant improvement/greatest upheaval,
- Considerable improvement/considerable upheaval, or
- Acceptable improvement/minimum upheaval.

The goal of a 25% reduction in cost within three years, one outcome of the middle course of action, was confirmed finally as the most reasonable path. The first scenario was rejected chiefly because of the reduction in staff numbers required.

In order to achieve its goal, DEC adopted TQM as the corporate-wide term for a set of four interrelated initiatives—"The voice of the customer," "six sigma performance," "cycle time reduction," and "benchmarking." All were aimed at achieving higher levels of customer satisfaction and providing competitive costs in all activities. The congruent initiatives rested on voluntary employee involvement, which in turn demanded leadership commitment and a considerable investment in employee education.

Each of these attributes is exemplified in the payroll department, where the manager is firmly committed to TQM through training individuals to work smarter, not harder. The business has become the internal benchmark for DEC and recently has been rated best in class (from a short list of 15 US and six Japanese companies) by a major firm of consultants. The operation is comprised of just 26 people. It pays 60,000 employees at 320 locations, 14% with individual checks, on a weekly basis. The manager knows the job plan for each of his staff; moreover, each plan is visible to all members of the group. Additionally, each individual is empowered to modify his or her own plan whenever conditions change.

All department members receive 10 days' training a year in total-quality-related techniques in order to help meet their personal objectives within the context of the department's three customer-oriented goals. Furthermore, all employees have a copy of the long-range plan, a 30-page professional brochure, so they have the opportunity to understand how their role contributes to attaining these goals.

DEC regards building co-reliance and combining continuous improvement efforts as a journey, rather than an event, the outcome of which will allow it to become a better listener and more willing learner in its selective drive to set new benchmarks. DEC stresses that it is vital for the focus of any benchmarking exercise to be both well chosen and grounded within the whole organization. This means a commitment to hard work and discipline.

Other lessons learned include the need for a framework for all benchmarking activity; allowing more time than is available; keeping objectives constantly in mind; developing actionable follow-through and, most crucial, having a dedicated sponsor.

The framework DEC formulated has four steps;

1 What to benchmark?
2 How is it done here?
3 Who is best?
4 How do they do it?

Only those factors that significantly affect the overall competitive position of the company are selected for benchmarking.

Throughout its activities, DEC stresses the importance of the systematic approach. This means ensuring correct understanding prevails from the outset. Positioning it in a proper context is a prerequisite before even thinking about taking the first step. Misuse, suggested the then-UK quality manager Mike Newell, arises from "advocacies without inquiry." That is:

- "We must reduce our costs by 25% (to equal the benchmark figure)."

Or

- "We need to let X (the benchmark) people go." (Consequence: Symptoms are tackled without understanding the cause of the difference.)

No one has prescient knowledge of what ultimately will decide which companies become, and endure as, best in class. DEC, however, lists three messages that could top the list for all aspiring organizations:

- Identify with a critical success factor that is customer focused.
- Get to know the related process capabilities really well.
- Benchmark in the context of experiential and action-oriented learning.

A customer-oriented organization cannot escape the long-term consequences of poor performance. Hence, DEC believes, the real success factors are linked with customer values, which in turn throw the spotlight on key areas where things must go right if the business is to prosper and flourish.

3. HEWLETT PACKARD LTD

A key feature of benchmarking, whether internal, external, or best practice, is its focus on processes as opposed to outputs. Rigorous analysis and understanding of internal processes, which frequently lead to significant performance improvement, also provide benchmarking teams with the foundation for their visits to "best practice" sites. Hewlett Packard is one company that has adopted process analysis as an essential part of its total quality culture and then used it to drive its benchmarking program.

Hewlett Packard was first established in the UK in 1961. Since then, it has grown to four divisions employing a total of 4,100 people, with a head office in Bracknell, Berkshire. This is the largest operation, employing 2,100; it is also the UK sales region office. Its operations include the Queensferry Terminal divisions based on the outskirts of Edinburgh. Other sites include Bristol for computer peripherals and a research and development office products division based at Crowthorne, Berkshire.

Understanding where Hewlett Packard is today and how benchmarking has helped its journey to total quality, requires a step back to the mid-1970s. At that time, one of its sister divisions, Yokogawa Hewlett Packard, based in Japan, had to compete against up-and-coming players in its home market. Its performance in most key areas was worse then than that of many of Hewlett Packard's other worldwide entities.

Yokogawa Hewlett Packard realized that bold goals were essential if the company was to stay competitive. In 1976, the division set for itself the objective of winning the coveted Deming Prize by 1983—a seven-year goal. To achieve this, it set out to improve its performance in every aspect of the business. The search for ways to do this led management to analyze everything it did and treat each step forward, no matter how big or small, with equal respect.

Not only did they reach their goal, but they did so a year earlier than planned—in 1982. This set the precedent that Hewlett Packard worldwide would follow, putting the company on the road to total quality control.

The philosophy of continuous improvement is now ingrained into every aspect of the company's operations. Despite or perhaps because of this, it realizes that businesses it is not even aware of also are improving constantly. It has realized that continuous improvement cannot proceed in isolation; it needs to be aware of what is happening outside the company to ensure that its improvements really keep pace with that of others.

The company's UK sales region constantly uses best practice benchmarking to monitor and asses practices and processes existing outside its operation. In this it sets an example in the technique for many of its European partner operations.

Internal benchmarking against other Hewlett Packard divisions and entities by the UK sales region is ongoing. This is not confined to a study of UK operations, but encompasses visits in Europe, North America, Japan, and Singapore. These "internal" visits have proved a useful learning experience in how to go about benchmarking, and many of the lessons learned have been applied to the often more challenging external benchmarking visits.

Hewlett Packard stresses the importance of identifying the process that will be the subject of the benchmarking study. Although this sounds a relatively simple task, in practice managers have found it one of the most challenging aspects of any benchmark program. Of great help has been the company's ongoing initiative on process management; this has resulted in the identification of a wide range of key processes and process owners.

Hewlett Packard's UK sales region has seen many improvement opportunities while undertaking external best practice benchmarking. Key areas of business, such as order fulfillment, credit collection, and sales finance have come under the microscope. In many cases, this involved multiple visits to a number of different partners.

In all cases, the teams sought to identify fully and understand their own processes before studying those of others. They found this considerably enhanced the effectiveness of the visits and resulted in the collection of large amounts of useful information. The common key to the teams' successes has been the fact that they all communicated their findings extensively and networked comprehensively, resulting in effective sharing of best practices.

While on visits, the teams concentrated on analyzing the "soft" narrative behind the "hard" performance metrics. Thus, a much deeper understanding of their partner's practices was gained: Importantly, they attempted to ascertain the intangible reasons behind the exemplary performance.

A measure of Hewlett Packard's success in its benchmarking programs is the increasing number of visits they *receive* from other organizations benchmarking *them*. Benchmarking is becoming part of the culture within the company; programs, rather than being driven from the center, often begin when individuals enthusiastically set them up themselves to tackle specific issues in their business areas.

Best practice benchmarking will remain ongoing at Hewlett Packard. The company recognizes the competitive marketplace is dynamic and ever changing. New nations and companies are constantly leaping to the forefront at the leading edge of industry. For Hewlett Packard, benchmarking is a means by which it can ensure that it is always aware of, and striving to adopt, best practices wherever they are occurring.

In 1995, Hewlett Packard Ltd's Finance & Remarketing Division, based at Bracknell in Berkshire, became the winner of the inaugural European Best Practice Benchmarking Award launched and presented by the UK Benchmarking Centre.

4. STATOIL*

It's one thing to be the first in your industry to successfully practice benchmarking. But the first in your country? This is a kudo that Norwegian-based Statoil can boast proudly throughout the benchmarking community based on the results of its first pilot study.

As a joint venture with British Petroleum, Statoil is the largest producer of crude oil in the North Sea, with operations in 18 countries. Established in 1972 in Stavanger, Norway, Statoil is the world's largest operator in offshore production loading. In 1993, it reported $12 billion operating revenue and $2 million profit.

Statoil's introduction to benchmarking occurred in early 1993 when it decided to improve productivity and customer satisfaction. The organization had heard of benchmarking for some time, but didn't act on this process immediately. That was until one of the executives took the initiative and asked the corporate quality department to look into what benchmarking was all about. The corporate quality manager, Bjorn Bentsen, said management knew American industries were involved in benchmarking, so a group traveled to the United States to visit three companies.

"Benchmarking is not as developed in Europe as in the United States, but it is coming—especially among the big industries," Bentsen said. "Some countries, such as Great Britain, France, and Holland, are actively taking it up as part of their continuous improvement. A few companies in Sweden have used benchmarking. Statoil is probably the leading company in Norway to do benchmarking."

LOOKING ABROAD

The visit to North America gave Statoil incredible insight on benchmarking and how to introduce it to the organization. Three individuals from Statoil visited New Jersey-based AT&T, New York-based Xerox, and Houston-based Amoco. Spending one day at each company, Statoil gathered information and benchmarking documentation. Bentsen said these organizations guided Statoil on how it should get started in benchmarking, and all supported the idea of joining the Houston-based International Benchmarking Clearinghouse.

---

* By Vicki J. Powers. Originally published in *Continuous Journey,* Summer 1995, American Productivity and Quality Center.

In December 1993, Statoil joined the International Benchmarking Clearinghouse as its first Norwegian member. It also invited benchmarking guru Bob Camp to conduct a top management seminar with 70 Statoil managers. He conducted a second seminar the next day for about 35 quality professionals.

"The top management seminar really made benchmarking take off in our company," Bentsen said, "as well as become focused on using benchmarking in a serious way. The top management initiative has really made lower management get interested in benchmarking."

JUMPING IN HEAD FIRST

Once Statoil created initial interest around benchmarking, it jumped into the process without looking back. Statoil created a benchmarking network that includes 16 people from different units, appointed by the managers of their units. These individuals, trained in benchmarking, meet four times per year for a full day.

The network members also helped write Statoil's benchmarking guidelines. These guidelines were written to ensure effective and result-oriented usage of benchmarking at Statoil. It describes how benchmarking fits in with continuous improvement, Statoil's benchmarking model, its ethics, and definitions of benchmarking.

The corporate quality unit, composed of four individuals, manage the network and continues to coordinate benchmarking activities for Statoil. The group also has established a Lotus Notes database that houses new benchmarking projects, requests from the outside, results, Statoil's guidelines, and the Clearinghouse Code of Conduct.

PILOT PROJECT KICK-OFF

Once the base had been established, Statoil determined the process for its first pilot benchmarking study: the Drilling & Well Technology process. The organization had focused on this area before benchmarking because of the specific need there, so it seemed natural to target this for the first pilot study.

In January 1994, a cross-functional group of six individuals formed the benchmarking team and spent 30–100 percent of their time on the study during the next six months. Audun Sirevaag, planning manager in Drilling & Well Technology, spent 100 percent of his time on the study as project manager.

"There was no formal training with the team when the study started," Sirevaag said. "We spent a lot of time in the beginning discussing what benchmarking is, since it's a very different level of knowledge. This gave us a common platform to learn from each other's knowledge."

The team decided to study the entire supply chain for casing, which is the material used in the drilling hole to extract oil. Statoil's annual consumption of casing is $65 million. The organization also wanted to reduce the amount of unnecessary casing it accumulated each year. Drilling operators always ordered an extra 10 percent of casing to be shipped to the rig—as part of an unwritten rule. An examination of records revealed that the real backup percentage ranged from 13 to 44 percent, with an average of 20–25 percent. And almost 100 percent of the backup of casing was returned unused. This resulted in 6,000–8,000 tons of unnecessary cargo per year.

"We asked employees where the '10 percent' came from and no one knew," Sirevaag said. "I think it's something we adopted from the Americans. Other operators in the UK follow the same rule, but don't know why. Because of the handling of the backup casing, about 20 percent of our return cargo from the rig was damaged."

STUDY DETAILS

The benchmarking team determined two objectives as the focus of its benchmarking study:

- Improve productivity and customer satisfaction with the supply of materials and equipment.
- Gain competence and experience in the use of benchmarking.

The team decided to benchmark its chosen parameters with others in the *same* industry by identifying operators in the North Sea with several offshore production platforms. It looked at five best practice companies in the United Kingdom and two in Norway, and selected four oil and gas companies as its partners. Bentsen said Statoil was very rigid in sticking with the Code of Conduct and in not revealing its partners. Statoil made bilateral contacts with participants so that companies involved didn't know who the others were.

"Working in a limited time frame and with limited experience, it was easier and faster for us to find good partners inside our industry," Bentsen said. "As a first project, I think it was easier, because it's easier to communicate with companies of our own kind. I would consider having someone outside our industry in future projects because I expect you'd find even better practices."

REVELATIONS FROM SITE VISITS

The site visits revealed three different ways organizations work with casing: two best practice partners followed the "outsource model," two partners followed the "consignment model," and Statoil used the "in-house model." Statoil learned quickly that its contracts with many different steel manufacturers created lengthy lead times and bad coordination with suppliers. The other models used one supplier or wholesale dealer. The team concluded that the outsourcing model had the best potential for improvements (Figure 1). The best practice is based on selecting the best elements from the different companies.

"The company who had the best process used the outsourcing model," Sirevaag said. "The wholesale dealer would place a large order for several operators, which caused the cost to go down. With casing consumption

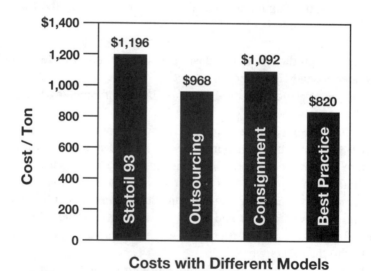

Prices per ton for an average string of casing

Costs with Different Models

FIGURE 1. Before benchmarking, Statoil's consumption was 30,000 tons. (Based on 1993 data.)

of 30,000 tons, it adds up quickly for Statoil. Standard delivery with this model is two days, versus five to six months for Statoil's process."

A CHALLENGING EXPERIENCE

Like every organization that conducts a benchmarking study, Statoil experienced some challenges along the way that added spice and variety to the project. According to Bentsen, the greatest challenge was understanding Statoil's process and identifying and agreeing on metrics. This contributed greatly to the end result in his mind, so it was important to work through.

LESSONS LEARNED

- Train the team before benchmarking.
- Create a balance between ambitions, time, and project resources.
- Avoid the "facts trap" of collecting too much unnecessary data.
- Form a well-composed project group.
- Understand that process mapping is time-consuming.

Serevaag felt one of the study challenges was expending quite a bit of energy explaining what benchmarking really is to management. Originally, management gave the team only four months to do the study, so Sirevaag felt they were continually asking for more time.

"There has to be a well-balanced relationship between the ambitions set for the project, the time available, and the resources one is willing to invest," he said. "At first our ambition was very high, and we started out too broad."

Implementation also has proved difficult for Statoil because of previous long-term contract agreements.

"It's not easy to implement large changes in a big organization, because we are stuck in agreements for probably the next two years," Sirevaag said. "Many things affect how far you can go with the changes. There is a distance between what we have learned as best practices and what we can implement within a short time frame.

A NEW FRAME OF MIND

Despite the hurdles, Statoil realized some culture changes and dollar results from its first benchmarking study. In terms of culture, Statoil:

- Thinks more in process terms.
- Sees the value of handling internal customers.
- Looks at the process as a whole process rather than parts.
- Recognizes the need for one process owner for each defined process.
- Looks outside to learn from others and is open to the idea that others are better than them.

In terms of improvements, Statoil has spent the past 10 months implementing its findings. Within the next 12 months, the organization is certain it can achieve these results:

- Reduce its annual cost of casing by $150 per ton—conservative estimate is $6 million savings a year.
- Reduce its variance by about 50 percent.
- Develop a "pipe wholesale function" internally to reduce lead time from five to six months to two days.
- Reduce backup casing 50 percent.

GROWTH OF BENCHMARKING IN EUROPE

To help its own future benchmarking endeavors, Statoil is looking forward to educating more European organizations on the benefits of benchmarking. Currently, Bentsen is involved in a Benchmarking Vision Group with the European Foundation for Quality Management (EFQM), which is interested in establishing a link to receive International Benchmarking Clearinghouse services in Europe. To fully utilize benchmarking in Europe, Statoil needs more companies in the area to benchmark with.

"Benchmarking is coming up as one of the most relevant improvement tools now, and I think it will be easier to benchmark when there is more interest," Bentsen said. "It's nice to be attractive to other industries who have contacted us and to be considered a serious company for benchmarking."

5. Johnson & Johnson Medical Inc.[*]

Henry David Thoreau represented the essence of simplicity in his language and lifestyle: "Our life is frittered away by detail. Simplicity, simplicity, simplicity!" A Texas-based surgical apparel company supports this same philosophy in its approach to benchmarking.

Not everyone agrees with the simplicity of benchmarking, but El Paso-based Johnson & Johnson Medical Inc. (JJMI), a division of Johnson & Johnson, purposely developed its benchmarking structure around simplicity. It recognized that "best-in-class" learnings change, too, so it's sensible to keep the process as simple as possible. JJMI's philosophy to benchmarking is definitely refreshing. At a time when many organizations spend large amounts of money, time, and resources to benchmark other best-in-class companies, JJMI has created its own successful method with short-term results.

"We chose not to be complex with benchmarking," said Michael Lewis, director of JJMI's El Paso/Juarez operations. "We chose to keep it simple for this belief: that we didn't have a long time to change. We believe that whatever we develop is going to change too, so why put all that effort into it, knowing it will change soon after."

A change for the better

In 1989, two Johnson & Johnson professional product organizations merged to create JJMI—Surgikos, with manufacturing plants located in Juarez, Mexico; El Paso, Texas; and Arlington, Texas; and Johnson & Johnson Patient Care, located in Sherman, Texas, and New Brunswick, New Jersey. While mergers are not uncommon among the 150 companies in the Johnson & Johnson family, they still require some initial adjustment uniting different management and manufacturing plants. As a result of this union, JJMI cuts and produces disposable surgical apparel and packs. Associates at the Artcraft facility in El Paso cut the raw materials and transport them daily to the three plants in Mexico for production. Once complete, these surgical products are sent back to El Paso for sterilization.

---

* By Vicki J. Powers. Originally published in *Continuous Journey,* April/May 1994, American Productivity and Quality Center.

After the merger in 1989, the former vice president of operations at Johnson & Johnson Patient Care empowered employees with the ability to do whatever was necessary to improve. Employees were faced with a freedom never seen before. Lewis, previously with Surgikos, jumped at the opportunity to make some changes, accepting the position of director of Mexico operations.

"I personally had a belief that we had to change," Lewis said. "And because I had that belief, and I had it very, very strongly, then we began to evaluate what we had to change."

Lewis described JJMI's situation in 1989 as "pretty bad." The organization was in a growth mode and unable to fulfill customers' orders.

"We weren't making our financial commitments," Lewis said. "We weren't making our production commitments. I believe that was the reality that hit us in the face to make us believe we had to change."

Lewis believes the common thread running through the organization was that *people* had a willingness to change. The organization started looking at the whole gamut of its business—from hiring practices to pay systems to measurement—and determined what it needed to do to improve.

A NEW DIRECTION

Lewis recognized during the organization's quality educational process that regardless of the quality "guru," the common themes among them focused on the customer, people, and education. He also noticed that every company he studied seemed to have a strategic plan. Although the plan may be sitting on an executive's shelf collecting dust, the companies he studied had a plan. Lewis did not want a stagnant plan for JJMI, so he asked himself, "How do I take this strategic plan or mission and deploy it in two countries and two languages?" The answer: Focus on a few very basic things. Again, simplicity played out as the answer for JJMI.

The organization created four critical success factors for JJMI with a mission of "superior responsiveness to customer requirements." The business is run based on these critical success factors:

- Customer-driven quality.
- Fast and flexible processes.
- Lowest cost.
- Total associate involvement.

STEP BY STEP: INCHING CLOSER TO BENCHMARKING

One of the first things JJMI did to improve the organization was to flowchart its business. Employees began looking closely at elements of work that were going into their activities. They broke into teams, by plant, and started eliminating the non-value-added tasks.

"We asked ourselves, 'Is this going to provide value to our customers or add value to our product?'" Lewis said. "We had to change the process to eliminate the non-value-added activities. And that is a continuing process. I'm not sure you ever finish that, because the business changes, products change . . ."

The organization also moved into benchmarking, which many associates describe as part of the Johnson & Johnson culture. In the opinion of Jack Morrison, Artcraft plant manager, JJMI has embraced the philosophy of not reinventing the wheel, but looking at others and "lifting" ideas from them. Morrison said associates understand what benchmarking is by seeing the results from it. "It has become self-perpetuating now," he said.

Lewis believes strongly in JJMI's method for benchmarking, as well, but he admits its benchmarking is different. And he's even asked himself, "Are we missing the boat?"

"But then I look at what we've done, and I see the results and the successes," Lewis continued. "We're not trying to be a perfect 4.0 on benchmarking. We may not be 100 percent perfection, but we're somewhere in the 90s on getting things done."

In the past three years, the organization has benchmarked 35 companies, such as Honda for its just-in-time deliveries by suppliers, Milliken for quality of design and manufacturing, and Federal Express for its on-time delivery and customer satisfaction. Teams are responsible for finding a solution to their projects, and for many teams, that involves benchmarking. Management has made it available by offering the resources and money in the budget, as well as a supportive hand to help.

"Benchmarking isn't a solution in or of itself, but one tool in a toolkit to excellent, world-class status," said Richard Brown, TQM manager. "We don't see benchmarking as a panacea. We didn't see a lightning bolt and all of a sudden start benchmarking."

One of the common misconceptions about benchmarking is that it's as simple as copying the success of another company directly into your own organization. Lewis has communicated to JJMI associates that they can go study a Federal Express- and Milliken-like organization and discover their best-in-class features, but they can't necessarily take their processes and put them in JJMI. They are not going to fit.

"So, our attitude and strategy is to go out and see what the concepts are—and take it to the next level and understand what those concepts mean and the ideas behind them," Lewis said.

ARTCRAFT LANDMARKS
(FROM JANUARY 1989 TO DECEMBER 1992)

Customer rejects	reduced by 85 percent
Leadtime	reduced by 83 percent
Customs cycle time	reduced by 72 percent
Manufacturing waste	reduced by 69 percent
Team participation	increased by 350 percent
Manufacturing costs`	reduced by 34 percent
Inventory	reduced by 60 percent
Supervisory personnel	reduced by 50 percent
Sterilizer utilization	increased from 56 percent to 98 percent (for a $4 million cost savings)
ISO 9002 certification	first Johnson & Johnson domestic company and first in industry

"GO, SEE, AND DO"

Lewis described JJMI's benchmarking mindset as "Go, See, and Do." According to Lewis, "go" only takes time and money . . . to "see," individuals see only what they want to believe. But "do?" That is the difficult part of benchmarking. People say they "do" things, but more often than not, it's just lip service. Lewis tries to instill in associates that they need to change and come back with take-aways—improvement opportunities. He asks them to make a list of 10 things they learned from benchmarking. From this list, he prefers the organization implement one strong change to make a legacy to the organization, rather than trying to accomplish all 10 items.

"We have to come back from benchmarking with a take-away," Lewis said. "It wasn't okay to go and see, and not come back and 'do' something—something you learned. Or, your take-away was you don't want to do that."

JJMI's benchmarking structure revolves around a seven-step process (see Figure 1) the organization adapted from many sources. This process is introduced to employees, along with the basics of benchmarking, as one component in their "Quality Journey" training.

One of JJMI's benchmarking efforts involved Milliken, which excels in two areas: measurement and associate recognition. Lewis, who attended this benchmarking trip, wanted to implement something he learned from Milliken when he returned. Milliken sponsors sharing rallies, where "the best of the best" teams make presentations and glory in recognition from peers and management.

"We came back and realized we could do the same thing, because we already had teams set up," Lewis said. "And we've done it three times so far. It's overwhelming what that has done for us in the organization, because people want to contribute. We don't have a three-ring binder and 100 pages on the Milliken recognition program. My belief is if we had done that, it would have taken longer to have our first sharing rally. We realized success very quickly."

Seven Step Process

1. Decide what to benchmark.
2. Analyze which variables should be measured.
3. Identify best-in-class.
4. Measure own performance.
5. Measure performance of the benchmark and create a gap analysis.
6. Develop plan to close the gap.
7. Implement plan and monitor results.

FIGURE 1

"Distinciones," the Spanish word for *distinctions,* is JJMI's version of Milliken's recognition sharing rally. Every two years, the four plants on the border shut down for one day to recognize employees with awards and a dinner. Only three teams per plant can present their successes to the audience, though 15 have already applied for the next sharing rally from the Artraft facility. On the off years, JJMI recognizes employees on a plantwide basis.

"'Distinciones' is a chance for teams to showcase their talents and results," Morrison said. "People want to be recognized, and they deserve it. Everyone wants to feel they earned their pay."

Lewis also visited Federal Express (as part of Federal Express' required tours as a Malcolm Baldrige National Quality Award winner). Lewis recognized two take-aways from this visit as well—Federal Express is sensitive to the customer and has incredible education and training programs. While many may not call this visit "benchmarking," Lewis does. In his mind, Federal Express is a winner, so they are considered a benchmark.

When Lewis attended this tour in 1992, the tour started at night when the bulk of its work is performed. Five thousand Federal Express employees come in at night to process one million packages in four to five hours. The planes take off, and the employees depart. What struck Lewis as he watched this process is "organizations must have happy customers."

"That was a real eye-opener for me—customer satisfaction is very important," Lewis said. "Because if Federal Express settled for only 99 percent on-time delivery, that would account for maybe 5,000 packages that didn't get sent on time to people who had to have their packages. So, we start trying to understand what customer satisfaction is to us and how we need to do that. And we're still trying to learn."

One method JJMI uses to ensure that it reaches customer requirements is to conduct plant tours with nurses, JJMI's major customers, several times a year. The majority of the 20–25 nurses per group are the decision-makers at their facilities. Nurses tour the JJMI plants in El Paso and Juarez, and in return, give JJMI feedback on products, environmental initiatives, and other appropriate measures. JJMI depends on this feedback and often makes adjustments as a result of customer concerns. Doctors and their operating procedures drive what JJMI produces. The organization develops packs and changes product lines to meet the needs of doctors, based on feedback from the nurses.

The visit to Federal Express also taught JJMI associates about training by showing them the capabilities that Federal Express has to train its associates. Lewis said JJMI personnel took concepts they learned from Federal Express, as well as others they had studied, and tried to determine where JJMI's niche was and how it fit its personality. At that point, the organization developed its programs and processes for education. One is the "Quality Journey" training all associates learn, as well as other courses that JJMI developed for employees.

THE HEART OF THE MATTER

What is it that keeps JJMI focused on quality and benchmarking? According to Lewis, it's one essential ingredient: the Border Quality Improvement Team (BQIT).

This management-level team is the leadership for the JJMI operation on both sides of the Rio Grande. In 1989, this team, composed of management and union leaders in El Paso and Juarez, formed with the belief that each week management needs to ensure that it is still following the same road map. A fixed weekly agenda with published priorities allows members to follow the strategic plan and focus on quality, costs, and benchmarking. These are important items for discussion, because JJMI believes they are all intertwined.

"Our quality initiatives are all driven by the BQIT—training, benchmarking, etc.," Brown said. "The key is that group of leaders meeting every week and agreeing on what their focus will be."

Most important, this leadership team serves a cross-functional team that sends a message to the rest of the organization—leadership by example. Lewis said the evolution of the BQIT will require some tweaking, but he believes it's entrenched in the culture now.

"The BQIT has been the common thread to bring the associates together who provide the leadership—in a very focused, concentrated way to make results happen," Lewis said. "Not to get together and talk or feel good about what we're doing but to continue to make change continue to happen. After our benchmarking studies, we'll come back and sit as a BQIT and talk about how that concept would apply to us. In some cases, it was an easy fit. In others, it wasn't fitting at all."

CHANGE IS IN THE AIR

As a result of JJMI's quality and benchmarking efforts, nothing seems to stay the same for very long. *Improvement* is the word of the day, every day. And one of the big changes involves the JJMI associates.

"People feel more empowered to do what they feel is right and not be penalized for making a mistake," Morrison said. "Associates feel they can question management, and they definitely have more pride.

"I love showing improvement! It's a matter of goal setting and putting a structure in place to improve. We haven't been faced with a situation that we couldn't do what we wanted to do."

Morrison's words have examples to back them up. Two of JJMI's most impressive recognitions occurred its second time around. The organization did not give up after one try.

Take, for example, the Premio Nacional de Calidad, Mexico's version of the Malcolm Baldrige National Quality Award. When JJMI's three Mexico plants, Surgikos, S.A. de C.V., entered the first year, they did not win. They weren't even finalists. But 1993 was a different story, one with a happy ending.

The Premio Nacinal de Calidad is given to organizations that succeed as a result of their efforts in continuous improvement toward total quality. In 1993, 85 organizations registered to apply for the award. From those, 12 were selected to prepare and send additional information. Eight of these companies received final site visits, and Surgikos was one of three winners. The president of Mexico presented the award to JJMI associates in November at the official presidential residence in Mexico City.

"It was pretty overpowering for me to go down to Mexico and have their president present that award to us with more than 1,000 people in the room," Lewis said. "It's an outside indicator that says we're getting this right. But we have to make sure we don't get arrogant and think we have arrived, because we haven't. We still have a lot of work to do."

Another recent accolade JJMI is pleased to tout involved *Industry Week* and its annual "Best Plants in the United States" recognition. JJMI's El Paso facility was named one of the best plants in 1993 in the magazine's October 19 issue. El Paso proudly follows the footsteps of Johnson & Johnson's Sherman, Texas, plant, which received the honor in 1991.

For its celebration, nearly 200 associates and their families gathered on the grounds of the Artcraft facility in El Paso for the presentation, reception, and plant tours. Bill Clarks, JJMI's president in Arlington, Texas, complimented associates on their teamwork and "willingness to try new approaches to increase productivity while better satisfying customers."

TURNING THE TABLES: JJMI AS A BENCHMARK

In addition to benchmarking inside and outside its industry, JJMI also has earned a reputation of its own as a best-in-class organization. Other companies in JJMI's industry have benchmarked several of its operations, including cutting room operations, customs/traffic operations, sterilizer operations, and materials management.

In customs, for example, the traffic-and-customs team has reduced the number of inspections to cross the border from 130 in 1991 to 10 inspections in 1993. Instead of taking 40 hours for one truck to travel across the border with inspections, it now takes two hours. These reductions are based on JJMI's special security agreement with U.S. Customs signed in 1992 to reduce inspection by 90 percent.

By working with such a large volume—30 shipments per day—the reduction definitely affects JJMI's bottom line. JJMI is the first organization to reach this level, so U.S. Customs recommends organizations to JJMI if they need assistance.

"The normal inspection rate is 10 trailers out of 100, which is rework and lots of scrap," Morrison said. "Our inspection rate is one trailer out of 100. You must have an ability to maintain accuracy. It's a matter of learning what the requirements are from Customs."

A SIMPLE ENVIRONMENT?

The work *simple* usually doesn't have a place in the environments of corporate organizations. They typically strive for complex language, complex processes, and complex organizational structures. Why has the philosophy of Thoreau vanished from '90s? In some respects, it hasn't. Organizations like JJMI act as reminders that life, business, and yes, benchmarking don't have to be complex.

"'Hard' may give you 100 percent and 'simple' may give you 89 percent in benchmarking," Lewis said. "But it's going to change anyway, so why does it have to be 100 percent. We just do it simpler."

6. SPRINT CORP.*

"At Sprint, we put benchmarking in the framework of total quality and process improvement—it is not seen as a stand-alone savior," said Jeff Amen, benchmarking manager. "We're not in the game of 'having,' but in the game of 'doing'—creating processes that affect the organization."

Sprint believes benchmarking should be used as a tool within strategic business process improvement and reengineering. According to Amen, it's the process of understanding what the organization does and what the critical components are. The underlying question is: Who does it and what can *we* do to become or remain the best of the best?

Sprint Benchmarking is an outgrowth of Sprint's total quality framework, Sprint quality, which started in early 1990. Sprint Quality's three essentials (phases) include teamwork, strategic integration, and continuous quality improvement. The organization determined that benchmarking was needed in the strategic integration phase to foster breakthrough thinking in areas that affect the customer. Sprint Benchmarking follows the methodology supported by the International Benchmarking Clearinghouse (IBC)—Plan, Do, Check, Act.

THE ROAD TO BENCHMARKING

"During the first year of benchmarking, I got two types of calls from employees," Amen said. "People asked, 'Tell me what our chief competitors do in this area,' and 'Here are six companies I want to talk to—get me in the door.' I had to tell people first that they weren't ready to do benchmarking."

Sprint developed a benchmarking training module and adopted the just-in-time approach to spreading the word. When management sees a need for it, teams are trained in benchmarking. That way, knowledge is not lost while employees wait to begin their first benchmarking study.

One of the most exciting benchmarking studies, according to Amen, focused on customer service in the consumer division. This group came to Amen in December 1993 to study processes that customer call center supervisors complete, such as attendance and personnel staffing. Amen worked with a core team of two to three people and helped with the ini-

---

* By Vicki J. Powers. Originally published in *Continuous Journey*, January 1995, American Productivity and Quality Center.

tial research. Others were pulled in who would need to see a best-in-class company. The group realized that probably the best practice for supervisors is to emphasize their roles as coaches, but that would require a culture change of the call center.

By the end of May 1994, teams had attended two site visits to other organizations. Teams were completely shocked by the answers they received to two questions relating to dress code and attendance policy. The attendance policy of one organization: "come to work." Requirements for the dress code: "wear clothes."

"We got the biggest whack on the side of our head by the answers to questions like that," Amen said. "We were surprised to discover their attendance policy was not volumes of pages like ours. We obviously had a long way to go to make it three words. This organization also didn't feel a need for spelling out a dress code, because they coached employees about what to wear."

From this benchmarking study, Sprint realized the importance of culture and the culture of trust. Once that is established, organizations can examine the appropriateness of its policies and technology.

Information from this benchmarking study has played a vital role in many organization changes within the customer service group. Regarding its processes, process measures are valid, understood, and reported on frequently. Standards are in place, but the ultimate decision is made by the front-line associate. In the area of technology, upgrades to intelligent workstations allow technology to be a tool rather than a hindrance. Intuitive and friendly interfaces permit associates to concentrate more on customer care and less on system operation. Regarding the interaction with people, coaching, training, and motivating replace controlling and reprimanding as key roles of leadership. This study also helped management understand how high levels of trust yield high levels of commitment.

"I am there to assist any and all of these organizations who are in varying levels of readiness," Amen said. "Benchmarking is a tool to get us 'out of the box' of telecommunications. It asks people to step back and look at the processes without the telecommunications lexicon that surrounds it.

"I ask employees how they would phrase this process if they were on the outside looking in," he continued. "This opens their minds in terms of research, and that's been the key to getting us out of the box."

Sprint has been involved in 10–12 benchmarking studies overall— some directed by Sprint and others through consortium studies and consultants. Throughout these experiences, Sprint has learned several important lessons. One key area is looking internal first before going outside

Sprint. Amen said they continue to be pleasantly surprised at what the organization knows inside Sprint. They now tie the pieces together from internal benchmarking before going outside.

Sprint also has learned the importance of keeping control of the scope of the project. Employees are more willing to participate if the scope is narrow, and it will be a much more focused effort.

Amen also described the importance of working with executive levels and process owners at the outset of any benchmarking study. He stressed the value of benchmarking networks, such as IBC or SPI, as an invaluable way to get to companies for benchmarking.

"Our whole two-year effort so far has been a big learning lab. In the next six months to a year, we will be hitting benchmarking full-force," Amen said. "We're probably at the point I had hoped by now."

What has enabled benchmarking to be successful at Sprint? In Amen's mind, it's the executive support.

"It's worked for us because of the executive commitment to allow it to be the rigorous process it has to be," he said. "For those in the organization who want a quick fix, benchmarking is not what they choose to do. It's not just the site visits or picking up the phone—there's the rigor involved as well. We've realized that we need to listen and get it down the right way."

7. GM SERVICE PARTS OPERATIONS*

It's not often that an operating group hits a home run in its first time at bat. But in the process benchmarking "ballgame," General Motors Service Parts Operations did just that.

General Motors Service Parts Operations (SPO) is a 26-year-old operating group under General Motors (GM) with roughly 14,000 customers and nearly 13,000 employees world-wide. It primarily provides parts and service to GM dealers for vehicles produced in North America. It also provides parts and service, through AC Delco, to the independent aftermarket that services GM vehicles outside the GM dealership.

SPO's beginnings with benchmarking trace back to the strategic planning organization that was the impetus to benchmarking. According to Amy Cannello, SPO benchmarking manager, who joined the Strategic Planning group in September 1990, one of her major objectives was to develop a process for benchmarking at SPO. Now it's considered on the vanguard of formalized process benchmarking at GM.

"Our benchmarking philosophy at SPO is that it's only *one* tool for process improvement," Cannello said. "We use it primarily for core processes that are strategic in nature, not tactical."

THE FOREFRONT OF BENCHMARKING

SPO selected the Product Release and Change System (PRCS) as its pilot benchmarking study in late 1991. This horizontal process begins when each vehicle division communicates the parts used in a vehicle to SPO and ends with creation of a schedule to suppliers. In non-GM terms, it refers to the process of introducing a replacement part.

The process and system that SPO utilized for replacement parts had evolved into a patchwork system over time. The process was completely sequential with a long cycle time, significant redundancy between activities, poor performance monitoring tools, and a poor expediting system. Specifically, there were four reasons why SPO selected this process as its pilot study:

---

* By Vicki J. Powers. Originally published in *Continuous Journey,* Summer 1995, American Productivity and Quality Center.

- High systems/operations cost.
- High level of customer dissatisfaction.
- Area of weakness from a competitive standpoint.
- Key success factor for SPO.

"Customer dissatisfaction within our GM dealer organization was a big issue," said Bob Olsen, manager of service readiness and head of the implementation team, "because they were unable to get service replacement parts on new vehicles when they were introduced. This became a real throttle from their perspective. In the late '80s, we averaged 50 percent readiness on parts, which has improved to 91 percent readiness in 1994 after benchmarking."

BENCHMARKING AT A GLANCE

The benchmarking team started the benchmarking process by documenting the process as-is before the study. Based on the sequential nature of the old process, the team could visually see the snag—one step in the chain could not begin processing parts until the previous one completed its tasks.

Next, the team set partner criteria—one of which was to select partners outside the automotive industry. Olsen said this proved a worthwhile decision, because they saw a high-level focus they wouldn't have seen from their competition. In his mind, sometimes it's an advantage not to be intimately involved in the process.

"We selected three organizations outside our industry as benchmarking partners after looking at about 10 companies," Olsen said. "We looked at similar processes from organizations that were more focused than we were. We quickly realized our whole focus was wrong. We were trying to improve cycle time. But in fact, the issue wasn't how fast the part is turned through the system—it's having new parts ready when the product is introduced. As a result, we changed our focus to measure how 'ready' we are when the product is introduced."

After the benchmarking team's first site visit, Cannello, team leader/facilitator, realized the team needed a data collection tool to ensure a consistent methodology for collecting data. In response, she created a site visit binder to help organize team members and keep the data together. The partner's binder was sent one month before the site visit with the following information: SPO information, project mission, code of conduct, quantitative information, agenda, and topic list. SPO team members receive a binder with the same partner information and a few additional pieces: partner and SPO questionnaires, selection matrix, and topic lists.

"The site visit binder was an invaluable tool to keep us focused and help us get the information we needed," Cannello said. "It's so important for teams to be well-prepared and schooled on the information already available. Unless the team is prepared, it's not going to leverage the advantage of process improvements the site visit company can offer."

ENABLERS

After the benchmarking team conducted its site visits, it recognized four enablers companies need to effectively manage the process of introducing new replacement parts. These included:

• Focus.
• Structure/Responsibility.
• Culture.
• Communication.

First, SPO recognized its partners had a consistent focus on product introduction date and didn't consider internal customer cycle time as a critical measure. The best organization used one report to manage the process, while SPO used 45. Some best practice companies even held product introduction until the service parts were available. The team also discovered culture was a critical factor that helps companies achieve a higher level of performance. This is accomplished by greater interaction between service and manufacturing who team together throughout the life of the product.

"A couple of the enablers were pretty obvious, but we might have missed the other two without the benchmarking study," Olsen said. "And those two were significant learnings. We learned we weren't measuring the right things, such as 'percent readiness figures.' And it wasn't until we calculated them that we realized how really bad we were performing as an organization."

IMPLEMENTATION

Throughout the entire benchmarking study, which took about seven months before the implementation phase, implementation was drilled as an important part of the benchmarking process. The goal was to implement as many enablers as possible, so SPO broke implementation into two phases: short-term implementation and long-term implementation.

"We purposely focus on short-term implementation within our benchmarking process to show progress and make things happen," Cannello said. "Short-term implementation gives people energy to implement long-term findings, especially for a pilot study."

SPO experimented in its first study by using a separate team for implementation after the benchmarking study was complete. This arrangement was more by chance than by choice. Because an implementation team was already assembled to develop a new system, this team waited for the study to end to begin its process.

"I recommend a 'cradle-to-grave' team for process benchmarking and implementation, rather than two separate teams," Olsen said. "We didn't have the profound knowledge that we do now. The continuity is lost when you have to restructure and reeducate the teams."

With the site visits complete in August 1992, the short-term implementation began in Fall 1993. Olsen said the organization was not ready to implement key enablers right away because the organization was commodity focused rather than vehicle focused. SPO required organizational changes that took time to put in place before implementation could begin.

The majority of implementation for the pilot study was complete in the first year. In two years, 15 of 25 enablers were implemented for the replacement parts process. The other enablers are considered "out-of-scope," because GM is structured differently from the benchmarking partners.

Some of SPO's impressive results go beyond dollar amounts. Cannello has seen many culture changes as a result of the benchmarking pilot study. These include:

• Increased acceptance for process improvement.
• Increased willingness to look outside the industry for best practice.
• More focus on process rather than systems.

Regarding the dollar savings, SPO has dramatically improved in many areas from 1992 to 1994:

• Cycle time has decreased from 54 days to 20 days.
• Service readiness, the new measure SPO captures, has improved from 73 percent in 1992 to 91 percent in 1994. The slogan in 1995 is "95 percent in '95."
• Optimum cycle in hours has dropped from 240 hours to 24 hours.

• Dealer satisfaction has improved from 92.5 percent to 96.8 percent.

Overall, SPO has saved nearly $2 million from its first benchmarking study: $1.8 million in operations savings and $48,000 in system costs savings.

"As an organization sees improvements, there's more and more buy-in from management and employees," Cannello said. "I don't see benchmarking going away at SPO."

Cannello's statement is right on target. In addition to completing the replacement parts pilot benchmarking study, SPO currently has 10 benchmarking studies in various stages. The organization also has added a second person, Christine Judd, to help Cannello facilitate its benchmarking studies. SPO also is developing a User's Guide to encourage team leaders to take more ownership in the facilitator role.

"After completing our first study, we have a much broader base of benchmarking knowledge," Olsen said. "We also have a better understanding of the process and are better organized for site visits. We're light years away from where we were in the early '90s with benchmarking."

12

MANAGING BENCHMARKING IN THE ORGANIZATION

BALANCING THE INTERESTS OF THE BUSINESS WITH THOSE
OF THE CUSTOMER
FOUR PHASES OF DEVELOPMENT

Benchmarking is one of a number of initiatives or tools that can be employed by companies undergoing a change strategy. As seen in Chapter 3, benchmarking usually links with the quality improvement and problem solving processes. Depending on the degree and level of change required these may include other initiatives such as Just-in-Time (JIT), Simultaneous Engineering, Statistical Process Control (SPC), Electronic Data Interchange (EDI), Total Productive Maintenance (TPM), Total Cost Reduction (TCR), and so on.

Whether benchmarking is the prime change motivator or is secondary to another initiative, it must be managed to ensure optimum effectiveness of both the process and its contribution to other management processes of the business—the planning and budgetary cycles, for example.

In progressing toward becoming "best of the best" in what is produced and in the processes and resources employed in providing excellence, companies will become more efficient in the use of (always scarce) resources. This may involve freeing up people, or capacity and/or producing more of what the customer wants.

Management must balance the interests of the company with customer needs while maintaining the "best practice" philosophy. All of which adds up to a difficult juggling act.

Ultimately, benchmarking is *continuous learning;* the more it is practiced, the more can then be applied next time. This makes it potentially very powerful. However, the benchmarking experience needs to be managed to ensure it is continuously recycled to complement the development of the company. Sustainable continuous improvement can be achieved only if the *status quo* is constantly challenged and excellence standards reset. Therefore, a company's approach to benchmarking requires constant attention and updating to maintain both the internal and external pace of development.

Consequently, benchmarking must be coaxed if optimum benefit is to be derived. The style and level of management involvement will vary according to the phase. Recognizing this at the outset ensures the appropriate groundwork while maintaining an overall perspective of the end goal.

For ease of explanation, the development of benchmarking is split into four distinct "ages." In reality these will overlap (see Figure 12.1) and often be confusingly intertwined. The main point is to recognize the trend and inject the appropriate management emphases to foster development. As with any initiative, management is required throughout with attributes having background support status during one phase and becoming predominant during others. Management expertise relies on knowing how to balance these to best effect.

PHASE 1: PUBERTY

This stage is characterized by:

- Confusion about the difference between competitive analysis and benchmarking, and when the former becomes the latter.
- A lack of commitment to the need for change and uncertainty about the efficacy of benchmarking to instigate it.

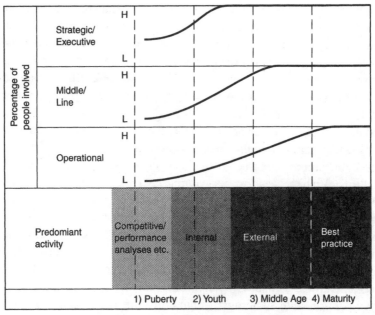

Notes: 1. Competitive/performance analyses frequently precede formal benchmarking either as a separate activity or as a means of establishing the company's relative standing prior to launching formal benchmarking.

2. The predominant activity will generally 'straddle' the transition from one 'age' to the next.

3. As benchmarking reaches late maturity many, if not all, these activities are likely to be going on at the same time.

FIGURE 12.1: Predominant benchmarking activity and management involvement during the four "phases" of development.

- A belief that despite all evidence to the contrary, a quick fix will still be possible.
- A feeling of just wanting to "check out how good/bad we are."
- A lack of conviction that the company will have the stamina to sustain a longer-term initiative.
- A lack of appreciation of the everyday consequences of adopting a benchmarking culture, e.g. openness and sharing.
- Fear that it may involve considerable effort and resource but not provide the right solution in the end.
- Concern about the strategic consequences of a benchmarking exercise.

All of these can be overcome by firm, positive leadership at the appropriate level, informed management aware of the consequences, and culture change brought about through benchmarking. The general rule is to keep all signals clear, concise, and comprehensible.

Whether benchmarking starts at the initiative and in the domain of the quality manager, or at strategic corporate level, solutions for optimum management will be the same. Benchmarking will require:

High level of commitment. Before any actual benchmarking activity can begin, somebody (the quality/customer service manager) or a group of people (senior executive team) must be firmly committed to the need for change and to benchmarking as one of the cornerstones for instigating it. The more strategic benchmarking is, the greater will be the demand for resources over time. Hence, it requires commitment at a commensurate level.

Enthusiastic vision and realistic interpretation. Change is always threatening. The more widespread the degree of change, the slower and more fragile the progress will be. From the outset, change will be more welcome if it is enthusiastically conveyed as something that is demonstrably for the better. The most realistic vision is one everyone believes they can have a part in growing, rather than one that is planted on them. Benchmarking, with its focus on best practice that already exists, must always be conveyed as a realistic interpretation of the future.

Conviction and clarity of purpose. The mission and objectives must be *understood* by all employees before a critical mass of support for change can be expected. It must be equally clear how they will be achieved through benchmarking.

Everyday language. People cannot achieve unless they understand. One of the problems that anyone "in-the-know" soon forgets is that some of the terms are specific and are not common phrases. As a rule of thumb, it is best to avoid short form (6-Sigma, SPC, QIP, PONC) as well as any phrase that needs explanation (customer service voids, sunsetting, deliverables, performance drivers, straw man models, and so on). If a common, everyday language is not installed from the outset, people throughout the organization will make assumptions and interpretations based on their perceptions. These will not necessarily concur with the organization's goals or even colleagues' perceptions. Misunderstandings will occur sooner or later.

Working definition. The early days of benchmarking will be characterized by; random visits *to* other companies; random visits *from* other companies; and no efficient process for capturing or sharing information. A working definition of the term itself *in the context of what it means to* *the organization* is needed to focus the activity. It is not necessarily the same for everyone. Merely adopting another company's definition is not the solution. Management must *think* what it means to their company. It must also be capable of enduring over a period of time. If it is not relevant in the context of the prevailing language and culture, it will have no effect on people's activities and will be soon forgotten.

Coordination. As awareness of benchmarking grows, there is a tendency for many small pockets of activity and experiments to spring up throughout the organization with numerous individuals or groups going off on forays or gathering data. While this is a sign that people feel personally empowered to improve their work situation—and is to be encouraged—the activity will be more effective if coordinated from the outset. It is not necessary to install intricate systems; it is preferable to select one or two approachable, creative people to act as catalysts and information channels. Their role is to know who is doing what and where, put people in touch with one another, stop individuals re-inventing the wheel, and generally help avoid duplication.

Training. The earlier people can receive education in the benchmarking technique the better. The temptation is to detail a few employees to find out more about whether this technique could be helpful, give them no training other than directions to the nearest bookshop or library, and expect them to return in a relatively short space of time with usable data and cogent arguments. It is easier to install good habits from the start than to cure bad ones later. Hence, the emphasis should be on the overall approach and how it can help attain objectives. It is better to instill an early awareness of th need for diligence in applying the plan, analysis, action, and review cycle than to focus too heavily on the individual steps.

PHASE 2: YOUTH

The most important management activity at this stage is drawing together all the threads and pointing the benchmarking activity in one direction. This includes putting in place the administrative mechanisms that will secure the long-term efficacy of the program.

In the early days of exploratory visits and internal benchmarking, the more activity the better (provided it is useful, coordinated, and informed) to grow critical mass for the technique. However, benchmarking almost always leads to change, and this must be managed, directed and focused. The more decentralized the organization, the greater the need for clear management, particularly if several business sectors are likely to prioritize similar processes for benchmarking at the same time.

The characteristics as this phase progresses are:

- Lack of priority.
- Confusing demands on resources.
- Growing conflict between desire for instant success and longer-term improvements.
- Differing levels of awareness and commitment.
- Differing degrees of reaction to the technique, ranging from resistance and rejection to acceptance and commitment.
- Number of different groups and interests involved.
- Conflict between personal and benchmarking objectives.
- Varying levels of training needs.
- Confusion over findings and their implication for operations or strategy.
- Uncertainty over degree of internal support, recognition, and reward for activities.
- Uncertainty about the level of external acceptance.

Particular emphasis on the following areas could "solve" many of these uncertainties.

Leadership. Someone must lead the overall process. This is preferably a senior executive with the overview to ensure that the initiatives fit with the direction and purpose of the strategy, and that they are prioritized to the mission, goals, and objectives. It will be the "leader's" responsibility to avoid conflicts of interest. The leader will be accountable to the board of directors and the benchmarking teams for trade-offs where necessary to make sure that the right things are done at the right time and in the best interest of the company.

Line-management commitment. Middle and line management are always in the "firing-line." At most, they can handle effectively only one or two changes or new initiatives any year. Each involves meetings, time for gaining acceptance, learning and installing new systems, procedures, documentation, and so on. Meanwhile, this cannot detract from the day-to-day work that must continue undisturbed. One of the most effective ways of securing commitment and gaining support at this level is to integrate benchmarking into management plans and objectives. This then sets the expectations that should be reviewed in annual appraisals. Inclusions should encompass:

- Which processes require improvement and why.
- Which organizations are believed to employ better practice in those processes.
- How many should be investigated.
- Number of best practices found, where and how.
- Improvement plans implemented as a result.

Training. General training in the technique should continue to penetrate through the organization during this phase to ensure a consistent message and understanding. It is also necessary to introduce more specific emphases. In particular, there is greater need to concentrate on progressing individual steps to produce usable findings. Usually this will involve meshing benchmarking efforts and findings with other total quality initiatives so they are supportive of and complementary to one another.

The findings from the planning and analysis steps may not always correspond to expectations. The second need, therefore, is to ensure that the presentations of findings are well informed and prepared. These must be thoroughly understood and comparable with the *status quo* before being reported. They may, for example, need to be tailored to the audience's personal business agenda. A skilled presentation often can do more than facts and figures to influence the decision to support further efforts or accept recommendations.

Training must move forward and be updated as expertise develops. Ideally, it should incorporate learning from benchmarking team members and case studies from exercises carried out. This helps keep development at a practical level as well as standardizing the technique, language, and methodology used. Furthermore, it promotes consistency and team-based learning.

Networks, facilitators, mentors. Throughout the second phase, it will be increasingly desirable to establish foundations for informal networks that will evolve as benchmarking advances. Internal mini-networks help to cross-fertilize views, ideas, and perceptions reducing the opportunities for tunnel vision.

Identifying and developing facilitators and mentors will promulgate use of the technique and reduce delay or confusion as people try to sort out intermittent queries and problems. It may be necessary to refer to outside professional help until sufficient internal expertise is developed. In this case, availability and lines of communication should be clearly "advertised."

Center of excellence. A proven way of providing consistent backup support is to formalize a center of excellence. This will include the internal facilitator and/or mentor. It may be one person or more. It can keep up-to-date on internal activity (including any historical evidence from bench-marking-type exercises), formal events such as conferences and seminars, and gather information at an informal level. Moreover, it is preferably linked to external networks to provide a filter, as well as the center, for benchmarking data and information.

The fundamental purpose is to relay relevant data and information (in and out) and provide a clearinghouse for all the company's benchmarking activity. As the link between internal and external networks, it is also the conduit for the two-way information sharing, which is vital in an increasingly competitive environment.

Guidelines and protocol. With the best will in the world, it is not possible to train everybody on all new developments as they occur. Different levels of expertise and varying degrees of activity confuse those "new" to the technique. It is beneficial to get the common message down in a simple, consistent, and easy to update user-friendly guide.

The outward, sharing culture that develops with benchmarking can run counter to previous behavior and provoke uncertainty or lack of confidence in people "new" to dealing with the outside world. This may become particularly evident as the activity devolves more to operational levels. Developing guidelines on information sharing, general behavior and presentation, the need for and nature of agreements, visit protocol, and so on is beneficial without being bureaucratic. In fact, a clear guide can *prevent* the buildup of bureaucracy. It enables people to get on and improve their processes, within a reassuring and consistent framework, without the need for installing complicated checks and balances.

PHASE 3: MIDDLE AGE

As activity moves increasingly toward concentration on external benchmarking, the following characteristics predominate:

- Growing concern for the impact of findings on strategic planning.
- Corporate "self-consciousness" arising from opening up to the outside world and letting others look in.
- Greater need for clarity of mission and purpose.
- Unwavering senior level commitment and support.
- Increasing emphasis on establishing a common purpose and corporate cohesiveness.

Emphasis on the following can help with these factors:

Integration with strategic change. At this stage it is vital that benchmarking is fully absorbed into the strategic planning process of the company. While it may be feasible to sustain numerous internal benchmarking activities, constraints on resources and the need for the "machine to keep on turning" make it unreasonable to focus on many external ones. By now, there is sufficient knowledge and expertise in the organization to be able to concentrate on key critical success factors and aim for significant improvement over the long term.

The demand for consistency with strategy becomes more important as external activity develops because of the impact on the image and reputation of the company. If the objectives, mission, and vision are sustainable and credible, the company's image will more likely be strengthened than diminished. Equally, the clearer and more simple the terminology used, the less likelihood of the meaning being distorted or misinterpreted by the outside world.

Maintain currency of information. It is important to find out what others are doing. Unfortunately, it is often the case that information, in journals or at conferences/seminars, is delivered with the benefit of hindsight. Thus, the views given are retrospective. As time elapses, the problems, barriers, enthusiasms, and lessons learned all diminish in people's minds. It is important to be aware of this and to find and create a dialogue or mini-network with companies *at the same stage of development*. If information is gathered solely from proven technicians or experts, it can be difficult to assimilate and even have a demotivating effect.

In the European culture, there is a tendency for companies to remain reticent until progress and improvement can be verified. This should diminish as more organizations incorporate benchmarking into their activities. Meanwhile, obtaining current information remains a constant challenge.

Greater integration with personal objectives. The process of incorporating benchmarking goals into personal objectives should by now be cascading through the organization to promote a common cause and purpose. The reward and remuneration policies should be amended gradually and weighted to reflect formal recognition for achievement. Certainly it will prove difficult to sustain enthusiasm and motivation for benchmarking if this does not happen.

Recognition. Benchmarking is invariably a team activity, and there should be formal rewards for excellence in team effort and achievement, as well as for individuals and team leaders. Successes and improvements always should be reported, but remember to keep the initiative "real" internally by including some anecdotal and humorous news coverage.

Over time, some successes will develop almost legendary status (as has become the case, for instance, with L.L. Bean and Xerox corporation). These can be developed to provide useful and provoking case studies for use in training.

PHASE 4: MATURITY

Not many companies have been benchmarking long enough to reach this phase. However, the predominant characteristics appear to be:

- The need to sustain motivation and energy for the approach, while maintaining the humility to recognize that improvement is still possible and desirable.
- Developing the flexibility to provide positive assistance to other organizations with the least possible interruption or disruption to the business.

Predominant management features during this phase include:

Rejuvenate roles. In all probability, strategic studies will continue over an extended period. Rotating the roles of team members and facilitators can help reduce the risk of people becoming desensitized to the approach. With certain key positions, such as team leaders, it may be preferable to rotate with another team rather than members of the same team. This will depend largely on the characteristics and strengths of individuals.

Keep it simple and fun. Just because an initiative has serious implications and consequences does not mean that all aspects must be conducted with strict and straight-faced dedication. Benchmarking will have far greater effect over the long term if fun, humor, and light-heartedness are encouraged. One company runs a regular humorous poster competition. Staff are asked to submit an entry that encapsulates the essence of benchmarking. The winning entry, in addition to earning a significant personal prize for the "author," then becomes the "Message for the Month." It is circulated in the company newsletter, on bulletin boards and any occasion where benchmarking is referred to.

Variations of this or a similar theme can be applied in most organizations.

Grow inside-out. Good companies recognize they can improve continuously. However, maintaining humility and the will to see where improvement is possible is not always easy. Inviting objective outsiders into the organization may provide a way through this. Regular, or even occasional, "meeting" events with customers, suppliers, and recognized proponents of "best practice" can present useful sharing and learning opportunities.

Best practice should not become a burden. Growing a reputation for best practice in any process is sometimes seen as a blessing in disguise. There are many thousands of business processes; every company has different critical success factors and strategic plans. Consequently, the number of companies benchmarking any given process, or likely to attain the accolade of "best" at any single process will inevitably remain small.

BENCHMARKING MISSION

Nothing provides a better foundation for benchmarking than a clear, succinct mission statement coupled with an equally crisp explanation of how benchmarking will help in its achievement. The following example from Royal Mail UK is one of the best:

"Our mission is to be recognized as the best organization in the world distributing text and packages."

Benchmarking is: "A structural process for learning from the practice of others, internally or externally, who are leaders in a field or with whom legitimate comparisons can be made."

Quality Improvement Process: "How can we do this better?"

Benchmarking: "How can we do this better by learning how others do it?"

In the maturity stage, therefore, the organization needs to be clear about how it responds to requests from others to benchmark a renowned best practice. A policy should be drawn up clearly identifying how and why to deflect industrial voyeurism while developing suitable partnerships. This must be communicated efficiently so that everyone in the organization can deal with requests and queries regarding benchmarking assistance.

Appendix

WORKSHEETS

Sample worksheets 1–7 relate to the text of the Planning Stage (Chapters 6 and 7). Worksheet 8 relates to the text of Chapter 9 in the Action Stage. They are intended as guides or prompts.

Worksheet 1

IDENTIFYING THE SUBJECT AREA – 1*

1. What business is your company in?

    ....

2. Write below three factors which are critical to your company for success in this business.

    i   ....

    ii ....

    iii ....

3. Which of these has the biggest influence on your company's performance?

    ....

4. Which, if improved, would have the most significant impact on customer/ employee/supplier relationships?

    ....

5. Which, if improved, would contribute most to bottom line results?

    ....

6. Which is of greatest importance to the successful continued development and future of the business?

    ....

---

* See Chapter 6.

Worksheet 2

IDENTIFYING THE SUBJECT AREA – 2*

Taking your response to question 6 on Worksheet 1, name below:

1. The major inputs

    i ....

    ii ....

    iii ....

    iv ....

    v ....

2. The major outputs

    i ....

    ii ....

    iii ....

    iv ....

    v ....

* See Chapter 6.

Worksheet 3

THE BUSINESS SUPPLY CHAIN*

Complete the boxes below for your business/function/job supply chain. Add further boxes if necessary.

```
┌──────────┐     ┌──────────┐     ┌──────────┐
│          │ ──> │          │ ──> │          │
└──────────┘     └──────────┘     └────┬─────┘
                                       │
                                       v
┌──────────┐     ┌──────────┐     ┌──────────┐
│          │ <── │          │ <── │          │
└────┬─────┘     └──────────┘     └──────────┘
     │
     v
┌──────────┐     ┌──────────┐     ┌──────────┐
│          │ ──> │          │ ──> │          │
└──────────┘     └──────────┘     └────┬─────┘
                                       │
                                       v
                 ┌──────────┐     ┌──────────┐
                 │          │ <── │          │
                 └──────────┘     └──────────┘
```

* See Chapter 6.

Worksheet 4

PEELING THE ONION*

1. Name a process with which you are directly involved.

   ....

   This is represented by 'X' in the diagram below:

2. Can you name the process at 'B' of which it is a sub-process?

   ....

3. Can you name the process at 'C' which is a sub-process of 'X'?

   ....

4. Can you also name processes at 'A', 'D' and 'E'?

   A ....

   D ....

   E ....

* See Chapter 6.

Worksheet 5

PROCESS STEPS*

Process name: ....

Charted by: ....

Date: ....

Details of method process steps	Type of activity	Measurement notes
1.		
2.		
3.		
4.		
5.		
6.		
7.		
8.		
9.		
10.		
11.		
12.		
13.		
14.		
15.		
16.		
17.		
18.		
19.		
20.		

* See Chapter 6.

Worksheet 6

SELECTING PARTNERS*

Taking as your starting point one of the processes identified on Worksheet 4:

Name:

  a) Two possible internal partners

  i) ....

  ii) ....

  b) Two possible external partners

  i) ....

  ii) ....

  c) Two possible best practice partners

  i) ....

  ii) ....

* See Chapter 7.

Worksheet 7

DATA COLLECTION*

Complete the form below for your data collection.

DATA SOURCE	RESPONSIBILITY ASSIGNED TO (NAME)	METHOD+	COLLECT BY (DATE)	CONFIRM COMPLETE
Internal:				
1. _____				_____
2. _____				_____
3. _____				_____
External:				
1. _____				_____
2. _____				_____
3. _____				_____

+ Specify whether phone, fax, survey, visit, interview, observation etc.

* See Chapter 7.

Worksheet 8

ACTION PLAN*

GOAL (a) ....

....

ACTION (b)	BY WHOM	DEADLINE	COMPLETE (c)
(List in sequence)	(Name)	(Dates/milestones)	(Yes/no) (If no, why?) (alternative course?)
1. _____	1. _____	1. _____	
2. _____	2. _____	2. _____	
3. _____	3. _____	3. _____	

NOTES: 1. Action plans show a desired state (a) at a fixed point in the future, together with realistic steps (b) for achieving this.
   2. Some actions at (b) will be parallel, some will be in series.
   3. Whenever 'no' occurs at (c) thorough review is essential particularly with regard to its impact on (a).
   4. Ensure alternative courses of action accurately communicated.

* See Chapter 9.

FURTHER READING

BOOKS

Camp, Robert C. (1989) *Benchmarking: The search for industry best practices that lead to superior performance,* American Society for Quality Control (ASQC), published by Quality Press.

Lascelles, D. M. and Dale, B. G. (1993) *The Road to Quality,* IFS Publications, UK.

Watson, Gregory H. (1993) *Strategic Benchmarking: How to rate your company's performance against the World's best,* John Wiley & Sons, Inc., NY.

Zairi, Dr. Mohamed (1992) *Competitive Benchmarking: An executive guide,* Technical Communications (Publishing) Ltd.

Zairi, M. and Leonard, P. (1994) *Practical Benchmarking: A complete guide,* Chapman & Hall, UK.

BOOKLETS

Best Practice Benchmarking by the Department of Trade & Industry, prepared and published under the Enterprise Initiative Programme. Available from DTI marketing offices.

An Introductory Guide to Benchmarking by ICI Chemicals & Polymers Ltd, available from Quality Library, ICI C&P.

ARTICLES/EXTRACTS/REFERENCES

Bemowski, Karen "AT&T's 12-step benchmarking process," *Quality Progress,* January 1991.

Bemowski, Karen "The benchmarking bandwagon," *Quality Progress,* January 1991.

Cavinato, J. "How to benchmark logistics operations," *Distribution,* August 1988.

"Competing with tomorrow," *The Economist,* May 12, 1990. (Ref. to "Why keeping your eyes open is not enough," by Gary Hamel, London Business School.)

Davies, Paul, "Perspectives - Benchmarking," *Total Quality Management,* December 1990.

Dumaine, Brian, "Corporate spies snoop to conquer," *Fortune,* November 7, 1988.

"First find your bench," *The Economist,* May 11, 1991. (Ref. to "Benchmarking world class performance," by Steven Walleck, David O'Halloran and Charles Leader - *The McKinsey Quarterly* 1991, No. 1).

Furey, Timothy R., "Benchmarking: The key to developing competitive advantage in mature markets," *Planning Review,* September/October 1987.

Hamel, Gary, Doz, Y. L., and Prahalad, C. K., "Collaborate with your competitors - and win," *Harvard Business Review,* January/February 1989. Reference to existing international collaborations.

Harlan, D. M., Jr., "Unleashing a plant revitalization," *The McKinsey Quarterly,* No. 1, 1991.

Lewis, B. C., and Crews, A. E. "The evolution of benchmarking as a computer performance evaluation technique," *MIS Quarterly,* March 1985.

McComas, Maggie, "Cutting costs without killing the business," *Fortune,* October 13, 1986.

Prahalad, C. K. and Hamel, Gary, "The core competence of the corporation," *The Harvard Business Review,* May/June 1991.

Quinn, J. B., Doorley, T. L., and Pacquette, P.C., "Beyond products: Services-based strategy,"* *Harvard Business Review,* March/April 1990.

Tucker, F. G., Zivan, S. M., and Camp, R. C., "How to measure yourself against the best," *Harvard Business Review,* 1987 (v. 87).

Walleck, Steven, O'Halloran, David, and Leader, Charles, "Benchmarking world-class performance," *The McKinsey Quarterly,* No. 1, 1991.

---

*Articles not specifically about benchmarking, but elements of the technique included.

USEFUL ADDRESSES

The Benchmarking Centre Ltd.
c/o Dexion
Maylands Avenue
Hemel Hempstead
Herts HP2 7EW
Tel: 44 01442 250040
Fax: 44 01442 245386

The British Quality Foundation
Vigilant House
120 Wilton Street
London SW1V 1JZ
Tel: 44 0171 931 0607
Fax: 44 0171 233 7034

The Centre for Interfirm Comparison
Capital House
48 Andover Road
Winchester
Hampshire SO 23 7BH
Tel: 44 01962 844144
Fax: 44 01962 843180

The Department of Trade & Industry
Kingsgate House
67-74 Victoria Street
London SW1E 6SW
Tel: 44 0171 215 7877 or Toll Free 0800 500 200

The European Foundation for Quality Management
Avenue des Pleiades 19
B-1200 Brussels
Belgium
Tel: 32 2 775 3511
Fax: 32 2 775 3535

Oak Business Developers
Long Gables
Templewood Lane
Farnham Common
Bucks SL2 3HJ
Tel: 44 01753 646854
Fax: 44 01753 646854

Profit Impact of Market Strategy (PIMS) Associates Ltd
7th Floor
Moor House
London Wall
London EC2Y 5ET
Tel: 44 0171 628 1155
Fax: 44 0171 628 2455

Benchmarking South Africa (BENSA)
National Productivity Institute
P O Box 3971
7th Floor Prodinsa Building
Cor. Beatrix and Pretorius Streets
0001 Pretoria South Africa
Tel: 00 27 012 341 1470
Fax: 00 27 012 44 1866

The British Quality Foundation
215 Vauxhall Bridge Road
London SW1V 1EN
Tel: 44 171 963 8000
Fa: 44 171 963 8001

Business Italy srL
Business International srL
Benchmarking Club Italy
Via Isonzo 38
I-00198 Rome Italy
Tel: 39 6 85300905
Fax: 39 6 853001046

The European Foundation for Quality Management
Avenue des Pleiades 19
B-1200 Brussels Belgium
Tel: 32 2 7791717
Fax: 32 2 7791237

Informationszentrum Benchmarking
Fraunhofer Institut fur Productionsanlagen und Konstruktionstechnik
Pascal Strasse 8-9
10587 Berlin Germany
Tel: 49 30 39006168
Fax: 49 30 3932503

International Benchmarking Clearinghouse
123 N. Post Oak Lane
Houston, TX 77024-7797
Tel: 713 685-4666
Fax: 713 681-8578

Oak Business Developers PLC
Truscon House
11 Station Road
Gerrards Cross
Bucks SL9 8ES UK
Tel: 44 1753 890434
Fax: 44 1753 894345

The SPI Council on Benchmarking
1030 Massachusetts Avenue
Cambridge
MA 02138 USA
Tel: 617 491-9200
Fax: 617 491-1634

Swedish Institute for Quality
Benchmarking Centre
Fabrikgatan 10
41250 Gothenberg Sweden
Tel: 46 31 351700
Fax: 46 31 7730645

INDEX